Writing
on the
Heart

Writing on the Heart

INVITING SCRIPTURE TO SHAPE DAILY LIFE

Gerrit Scott Dawson

Illustrated by Kelly Wood

UPPER ROOM BOOKS

Writing on the Heart
Inviting Scripture to Shape Daily Life

Cover calligraphy and design: Paul Shaw
Interior design: Charles Sutherland
First printing: April 1995 (5)
ISBN: 0-8358-0713-4
Library of Congress Catalog Card Number: 94-61265

Printed in the United States of America

To
Lois and Scott
Jay
and Willie
Family Written on the Heart

Contents

Introduction

❧

Welcome dear book, soul's joy, and food! The feast
Of spirits, Heaven extracted lies in thee;
....
Thou art the great elixir, rare, and choice;
....
The Word in characters, God in the voice.

Henry Vaughan, "H. Scriptures"

Why is it so difficult for us to live as people whose lives are shaped by the words of scripture? People readily agree that the Bible is an essential book. Yet we struggle to find time for reading it. None of us would like to be tested on how many verses we have committed to memory. And though we may feel comforted on those occasions when we do read the Bible, we have difficulty making connections between those sacred words and daily life.

In rare moments, we may grasp the relevance of a passage for us. We may be convicted by a sermon or receive a moment of insight in a Bible study group. Some daily meditation on a verse may shimmer with meaning in that instant. And we exclaim, "The Word applies to life!" But then we enter the pace of our activities and forget to think about what we received. Life intrudes upon us. In the heat of the moment, if we remember it at all, we can't seem to recall why the passage was ever so important to us.

What are we to do? We know that scripture is critical to our growth as Christians. We are fascinated with this book that a poet has called "a mass of strange delights." But we are also repelled by it. The words are too difficult, and we are usually too tired. It is doubtful that we will ever memorize many passages. Nor will many of us take extended retreats during which we meditate in silence upon the holy words. We just don't have time or inclination. We need a way to work with the Bible that takes account of the contradictory impulses within us.

As soon as scripture came into existence as commandments written on tablets, God's people have had to struggle to get the words off the page (or stone!) and into their hearts. Perhaps the old story from Deuteronomy can be of some help.

That It Might Go Well with You

Moses called the people together and gave them the commandments he had received from the Lord. There was no Bible at the time, but from the account in Deuteronomy we can begin to understand why it is so difficult and so important to know the words of God. Moses told the people of God's desire for them, "Oh, that their hearts would be inclined to fear me and keep all my commands always, so that it might go well with them and their children forever!" (Deut. 5:29, NIV). The purpose of the commands, then, was to enable God's people to enjoy their lives in many years of prosperity. We can glean from this that the Bible, as God's word to us, has been given that it "might go well with us." The scriptures are a source of abundant life whose springs are in God.

The Lord knew, however, that our tendency is to forget to keep our buckets filled from the springs, particularly when life is going smoothly. So Moses warned the people, "When you eat and are satisfied, be careful that you do not forget the Lord" (Deut. 6: 11-12, NIV). Learning the Bible is hard work; relating it to daily life is even more difficult. As long as things are reasonably good, we naturally put off doing the tough task. But when the inevitable changes in our circumstances occur, our resources are shallow and we are far from the source of renewal.

So Moses told the people to learn the words of life first, and he put the people on a program for keeping the commandments in the forefront of their daily activities:

> These commandments that I give you today are to be upon your hearts. Impress them on your children. Talk about them when you sit at home and when you walk along the road, when you lie down and when you get up. Tie them as symbols on your hands and bind them on your foreheads. Write them on the doorframes of your houses and on your gates.
>
> Deuteronomy 6:6-9, NIV

The people were to keep the words of the Lord running through their minds all the time. Moses asked them to be in constant conversation about them. In this way, they would keep God's words in their hearts. In the Bible, the heart is not only the center of emotion or the essential organ of the body, it is also the source of will and thought from which all our actions arise. Moses wanted the people to write God's commands into the very center of their beings.

Why Is This Work So Important?

C. S. Lewis echoed the words of Moses in his book *The Silver Chair*. A young English girl named Jill found herself on the edge of the magical land of Narnia. The great lion Aslan, who is a figure of Christ, appeared to give her an important quest. To accomplish it, she would have to watch for four signs along her way and then perform the tasks associated with each sign. Her life and the life of Narnia depended on her. Just before sending her into Narnia, Aslan told her:

> But, first, remember, remember, remember the Signs. Say them to yourself when you wake in the morning and when you lie down at night, and when you wake in the middle of the night. And whatever strange things may happen to you, let nothing turn your mind from following the Signs. And secondly, I give you a warning. Here on the mountain I have spoken to you clearly: I will not often do so down in Narnia. Here on the mountain, the air is clear and your mind is clear; as you drop down into Narnia, the air will thicken. Take great care that it does not confuse your mind. And the Signs which you have learned here will not look at all as you expect them to look, when you meet them there. That is why it is so important to know them by heart and pay no attention to appearances. Remember the Signs and believe the Signs. Nothing else matters.[1]

Introduction

We may compare the signs taught to Jill with the words of scripture given to each of God's people. Lewis described precisely the biggest difficulty we have with working with the Bible. The signs do not look the same in daily life as they do in the pages of scripture. In the Bible, God often talked to people directly. We seldom hear such a voice. People in the Gospels were healed instantly; our healing may take years. The right and wrong choices with all their implications seem apparent in Bible stories; we muddle along. If only the air of daily life were as clear as on the mountain. But it never is.

So, as Lewis acknowledges through Aslan, we need to know the signs by heart so we will recognize them in different forms. As Moses told the people, we write the words of scripture onto our hearts and keep them constantly active in our minds so that we will be able to see the connections with daily life when they arise.

A Method for Writing on the Heart

Such work is not easy. Through the pages of this book, I hope to provide you with a method that will guide you gently into some stories from the Bible. We will be considering four passages from the Gospel of John. Once we have entered the realm of the stories, I will attempt to guide you back out into your daily life with a fresh experience of how the passages apply to you. If the process works, when you have finished this book you will have written these stories of Jesus onto your hearts. His words and actions toward people long ago will be precious gifts to you now. And you will have a pattern to follow in your own work with other stories.

I have provided a pair of chapters for each story. (The exception is the Lazarus story, which has been given two pairs.) In each case, the first chapter of a pair will consider the feelings and thoughts of the characters who met Jesus. The second chapter of a pair will attempt to draw the connections between the world of the character and the world of our daily lives.

These are the paths I will invite you to take with me:

1) Explore the passage through an expanded story. The Bible stories are written in very compact, outline form. Few of us these days are skilled at meditating on them in silence until the rest of the story is filled in. So I will be offering more words as a way to unpack these stories, providing a style for active, restless people to linger over the feelings of the characters.

I have tried to limit my imagination to the scope of the biblical text. There is no way to know if my expansions are accurate; but I hope, at the least, that they will not be glaringly improbable speculations.

Through these expanded stories, we will seek to identify closely with the three women and three men whom we will meet from the Gospel of John. It is my belief that the inner dramas of their lives will be very similar to the inner dramas of our lives. Only the external form is different; therefore, their thoughts and feelings will be similar to the thoughts and feelings we have had. By entering their experience through our imaginations, we will begin to discover the deep associations between the people in the Bible and us. These story chapters include a prayer written in the voice of the character. So I will invite you to pray as if you were the person in the story.

2) Invite Christ's response to the characters to be his response to us. The second chapter of each pair contains reflections on how the biblical passage relates to contemporary life. We will attempt to fasten Jesus' words to our own situations. For instance, we will claim his healing power for the areas in our lives that correspond to the needs of the people in the stories. Or, we will bind to ourselves the forgiveness he gave a sinner as if it were to us.

To help deepen this identification, prayers toward the end of these chapters make the link between the lives in the Bible story and our lives. These are followed by short poems that can be used for claiming the words of Christ as words to us.

3) Reflect upon a symbolic emblem of the story that can be used in daily life to rekindle our encounter with the story. At the conclusion of every chapter, artist Kelly Wood has provided an emblem that allows us to consider the meaning of the story through art. Each emblem depicts an image from the story and highlights some significant words of Jesus from the scene. Through these symbols, we can understand the stories as events that happened once in history during the wondrous days when Jesus walked the earth, and we can discover how their meaning continues to reach into contemporary life. My hope is that these emblems will be a starting point for you to make your own symbols out of paper, clay, aluminum, or other media. This is a way we may both deepen our interaction with the story and ensure that we carry it forward into daily life.

These three paths have arisen from ancient traditions of working with scripture. (See the Appendix on page 145 for more details on these traditions.) One need not be a scholar in order to enjoy them. My hope is to employ them in fresh ways that take account of our contemporary time demands and life situations. I believe, however, that their value will be more apparent after you have worked with the stories yourself. Also, at the end of the book there are questions for further reflection, which may be used individually or in groups.

In these pages we will be attempting to write scripture upon our hearts. I hope the words and methods described will prove to be adequate writing instruments for you. I wish you courage and fortitude in the journey, and I thank you for being a companion along the way.

Note

[1] C. S. Lewis, *The Silver Chair* (New York: Collier Books, 1971).

One

❦

Getting Up

This is the thankful glass,
That mends the looker's eyes: this is the well
That washes what it shows.

George Herbert, "The Holy Scriptures (I)"

The story of the Healing at the Pool is found in John 5:1-15.

Early in the morning they lifted up the tiny bed on which he had slept. The night had been long and fitful as usual. There wasn't much need to rest when all he did was lie on that filthy pallet all day. It took three family members to hoist him: his uncle took the two poles on the front; his aunt and their son each took one of the back poles. They carried him on his bed out the front door.

He could hardly remember mornings beginning any other way. Every day was the same. After a simple breakfast of porridge, and sometimes a bit of fish, they left their small home and went to the Pool of Bethesda. They laid down the pallet at his usual spot, scarcely fifteen feet from the water's edge. There he joined the crowd of regulars who spent their days at the pool.

The pool had long been revered for its curative powers. Five columned porches had been built around the water. Within these colonnades lay hundreds of people with disabilities. They came every morning and waited for the moment when the pool began to bubble vigorously. It was said that the first person who entered the pool after its waters were troubled would be healed. The rumor was that the bubbles were caused by an angel touching down with healing in his wings. So whenever the disturbance occurred, all those around the pool made a grotesque scramble for the waters.

Once in a while, the legend seemed to be true. A man who had been crippled would leap from the water and declare that he was well. A woman with a tremor would run joyously and steadily out of the pool toward her home, singing alleluias. But most times, nothing happened. The sick just struggled back to their beds.

This man, however, had never made it first to those waters to test the theory. No one stayed with him at the pool, and he couldn't manage even those few yards by himself. Twice, years ago, he had tried. But heaving himself off his pallet and dragging his useless legs toward the water had left him exhausted. He was caught midway between the water and his bed, too weak to go in either direction. The memories of lying helpless in the dirt and the heat were so humiliating that he seldom thought of it.

These days, these years, he contented himself to lie all day on his bed and allow the hours to drift from cool morning through blazing midday back to the cool of the evening. When the day's work in the outside world was finished, they would come and get him. Once again they would lift up his mat on its poles and carry him to the house.

Often, he did not know one day from another. At the end of the week, though, the Sabbath would arrive and mark the time as different. No one was allowed to do any work from sundown the day before the Sabbath to sunset on the Sabbath. So he would stay at the pool all night. A few others who had busy relatives would stay as well. During these nights, the others would pull at his nasty blanket, hoping to get a little more warmth from its shredding threads.

This was the way of life for the man. For thirty-eight years he had been unable to use his legs. Palsy, some called it. A demon, declared others. He didn't know why or how it had begun. But shortly after his thirteenth birthday, not a month after he had supposedly become a man, he couldn't take another step.

In all that time he had never done a day's work, gone to the synagogue or even to the market. He had never taken his place in the deliberations of the other men about life in the village. No one asked his opinion. He knew plenty of village talk from his hours with the other persons by the water. But his relatives didn't want to hear. At night, after he was fed and cleaned up, they tried to pretend he wasn't there. The man felt like he was a chore on par with milking the cows or banking down the fire. The only times he could engage his relatives were when some complaint related to his condition would garner an extra moment of attention.

For a long time he had been angry with his relatives. He had thought someone should stay with him at the pool and help him down to the water when the angel came. He cursed them for being so busy, for giving him over to God's care, as if God would do something without human cooperation. He had learned, though, that his anger made them feel guilty; and guilt made them angry, so they simply neglected him more. No, he couldn't show them his rage if he hoped for attention. He just had to be sick and needy whenever they looked his way.

For several years, he had even wanted to be well. He held out hope that he would walk again, contribute to the town's life, maybe even marry and have a family. He had prayed fervently. Through long nights and the endless sameness of the days, he prayed: "Oh God, save me! Make me well! Heal me!" But nothing had ever happened. He began to believe that God had meant him to be an invalid. Change was not possible. Something he had done had brought this on himself, though he could never pinpoint anything. Perhaps it was his parents' fault. The same sin that brought their untimely death had perhaps cursed his life. Mostly he thought that God had just decided to use him as an example. He was God's victim.

During these forsaken days, all hope for a normal life was gone. He gave himself completely to the rhythms of his illness. As long as he was sick, nothing more could be expected of him. At least they had to change his bed clothes once a month. And he never let them forget to wrap his bread and cheese in a napkin and fill his skin of wine before they took him down to the water.

Some of the men and women by the pool were regulars like he was. Occasionally, he would talk with them to get the latest local news. But mostly he detested them. They reminded the man too much of what he had become. All the nasty labels he had used in childhood cruelty came home to haunt him. He was a gimp, a nuisance, a waste of perfectly good space. He was so dirty and foul in appearance that he would have kept his own children from getting near such a man.

So he lay on his pallet day by day. Once in a while he talked; every now and then he got angry and added to his barrel of bitterness. But mostly he just floated through the days being, fully and simply, an invalid.

A New Possibility

On the day that Jesus passed by the Pool of Bethesda, a particularly large crowd was there. It was near the time of a feast, and many people had brought their sick to the waters. They told the invalids that it was with hope for a cure. The man knew that this place was a convenient drop-off for inconvenient people.

Jesus surveyed the multitude of sick. He had the power, of course, to heal them all. But he seemed to be picking and choosing. Somehow, his eye fell on the man who was dozing on his pallet.

Jesus inquired and discovered that the man was one of the old-timers here. He had been by the pool for thirty-eight years. Jesus walked over and stood by the pallet. He looked long at the man, his eyes probing deeply.

"Do you want to get well?" the Lord asked him.

The man's reply was ready. What the man heard in Jesus' question was "Why are you still sick; why are you here?" He thought it was a question about whether or not he should be well. The man had learned ways to justify his illness long ago. It was the fault of those neglectful relatives. "Sir, I have no one to help me into the pool. When the water is troubled, someone always gets there before me."

Usually that stopped the curious. It made them feel that if

21

they really cared they would wait there with him and talk to him. If he really mattered, they would get him to the pool first when it bubbled. But no one had ever accepted the challenge. He was too heavy, too dirty, too loathsome to be with. And what would they do if he actually did get to the water first and wasn't healed? Then they'd have to do something else with him. So most people agreed with him that it was a shame, and how sad that God had made him an invalid.

Jesus didn't say a word for a while. And the man thought. Jesus hadn't asked him to make excuses for being an invalid. Jesus wanted to know if the man wanted to be well—as if such a thing were possible. It had been years since the man had thought of that possibility. He felt the tingle of anticipation rise within him. *I thought that part of me was dead! What's happening?* Fear came upon him. This Jesus looked like he expected something. No one had expected anything of him in years.

Then Jesus, never dropping his gaze, spoke deliberately, clearly. "Get up. Take your pallet and walk!"

Suddenly, there was no question about whether or not he could do it. He felt life in his dead legs, strength coursing through forgotten muscles. It terrified him. He had to decide, right now, if he would remain an invalid or get up. He didn't know what he wanted to do. But there was enough authority in that voice to make him move. He got up. He took his pallet under his arm and left the pool.

Jesus slipped away after that. When the man looked for him again, he was gone. He had been so astounded that his legs worked and that he was upright, with blood rushing in his head, that he had not even thanked the man.

Getting Up

A New Life

But what was he supposed to do now? He only knew one kind of life. He hadn't even seen the world from a standing position in thirty-eight years. The stimulation was overwhelming.

Fortunately, his long dormant faith awakened. Surely this was a miracle of God. So God did remember him! The requirements of the law dictated that someone who had been healed should go straightaway to the temple for cleansing. That gave him enough direction to keep moving.

As he walked, the man felt that health stretched out before him in a feast of imagination. The years could bring a family, a trade, a place in the world, joy. Possibilities flew at him even as the sights, smells, and sounds of the daily world rushed upon his senses. He was exhilarated—and terrified. Could he do it? After all this time could he stop being sick?

His reverie was interrupted as he approached the temple. Some of the Pharisees saw him walking with his bed under his arm and said, "You! It is not lawful to carry your bed on the Sabbath. That is more work than the law allows. What is the meaning of this?"

It had been so long since he carried anything that it never occurred to him that he was breaking the Sabbath. But the years of his illness had taught him how to shift conversations away from any personal responsibility. "The man who healed me is the one who told me to take up my pallet and walk. Who was I to argue?" When he didn't know the name of his healer, the authorities left him alone.

Later on, Jesus found him in the temple. The Lord came right up to the man and said, "See, you are well. See that you sin no more lest something worse befall you."

He didn't know what to do with himself then. He couldn't understand the words, "Sin no more." What was his sin? He had been a victim. How could he have done anything wrong as an invalid? Jesus was gone again before he could ask questions. But the words stuck in his mind. There was something he was supposed to stop doing.

One thing he had learned as a dependent was not to anger those who cared for you. They held all the cards. He figured the Pharisees would leave him alone if he told them who had healed him on the Sabbath. "It was the man named Jesus," he said. He wondered, though, if he had done the right thing when he saw the way they took off to find Jesus.

"See, you are well." He could hardly believe it. But perhaps that is what Jesus meant. His work now was to believe in his wellness and to stop believing in his illness. It was time to carry the pallet and not lie on it. He *was* well. Jesus had confirmed it. The man didn't know much about living as a well person. But he knew there could be no going back. His work was to choose to accept what Jesus had given him, every moment of every day. "Sin no more." Stop thinking of yourself as an invalid. "See, you are well." Hold onto the gift of God and live from it. Pick up the pallet, throw it away, or stash it in a storeroom; but never lie on it again. See, you are well.

Praying with the Man by the Pool

In order to identify with a biblical character, it is helpful to try on prayers from the character's perspective. I invite you to pray these prayers as if they were your own, as if you were the man by the Pool of Bethesda. I hope you will then be moved to compose your own prayers.

Getting Up

I

Lord, I cannot help but see into heaven,
On my back every hour of every day.

But the heavens are declaring
Nothing. I see no more than sky.

Where are you? Where are they? Why
Are they so late today? Don't they
Know I have needs? Don't you?

I am locked upon this pallet
As surely as the prisoner in chains.

This bedding reeks, but it is mine.
It stinks of the illness which is I.
Smelling of neglect, it effuses an urgent
Cry for care that no one can heed.

There is nothing I can do about it.
Isn't that right?

Surely you expect nothing of me,
When you have given me so little.
O Lord, I cannot help but see into heaven,
On my back every hour of every day.
But the heavens are declaring nothing.
Why are you so silent? Will you not
Speak a word of abandon, that I may be
More than this illness declares I am?

II

No, I do not want to be well.
Aren't you a little late?
I have a note from the doctor.
You know perfectly well there is
No one to help me to the water.

But you!
You reach into places
I had forgotten,
Evoking memories older than the
Memory that fails me.

You! You call forth health
In the midst of my illness.

You bid me rise from this bed—
Which I love, which I hate,
Which I love—and walk!

Very well, I am up,
Pallet in hand.
On my way I do not know where.

Oh, I do spring in this walking!
But the busy world is wide,
And my old bed is so safe.

You must understand that
I need you to declare me well
Again and again, yes every day,
If I am to live as more than I was.

Getting Up

An Emblem for Faith

On the next page is a symbolic emblem that was created after reflection upon this story. I invite you to spend several moments meditating upon it. Consider the location of the event in a definite, real place. This scene really occurred! Ponder the words of scripture chosen from the story. Consider how they communicate something central about the event, and how they give meaning to life today. Reflect upon how the story is rendered through the art. Allow the emblem to carry the story's meaning to you.

Two

Learning to Walk Again

Thou art all health, health thriving till it make
A full eternity.

George Herbert, "The Holy Scriptures (I)"

The man at the Pool of Bethesda had lost the will to be well. He had been so daunted in all his attempts to receive healing that he reached the place where he actually feared being able to walk again. We too may suffer disability in body or soul and lose the will to get better. In fact, we may fear the very wholeness we crave. Spiritually, then, we may become paralyzed. We may be unable to get any further than we have for the last "thirty-eight years." Some chronic problem may be blocking our ability to deepen our love for God. This disease may prevent us from finally accepting ourselves as God's beloved children. It may thwart our efforts to give to others in caring ways.

Some of us have a chronic weakness in our devotional life. We cannot get beyond superficial prayers and formulaic interpretations of the Bible. Trusted people have told us of God's nearness, and we believe them; though the times of actually sensing the divine presence have been rare. Fits of guilt drive us to live more constructively, but old habits always get the better of us just days after a determined start. We may live with an unspoken fear that God is poised to send us into the most uncomfortable situation imaginable. This indentured service, we believe, would be just deserts for our years of inadequacy. If we open ourselves to God, the call to the terrible task will surely follow.

Others of us find that we can never quite get our lives together enough to be of any use to anyone else. There is always one more horrendous day at the office or one more crisis in a relationship from which to recover. There is one more project at the house that just has to be done or one more weekend needed for "personal space" to "process the week." We can't ever get enough rest to have energy for people beyond our little circle. We can never quite get organized. Perhaps we fear getting involved to the point that we become responsible for another's well-being. The flood of needs in the world is overwhelming, and we fear being swept away if we get too near it.

Still others are afraid of their hearts. We are trapped in our minds where questions run roughshod over beliefs. All the standard unanswerable doubts work to keep God at bay: suffering in the world, hateful behavior among Christians, worrying about people who don't believe as we do. Of course, these issues pose difficulties for all Christians. But for some of us, beneath the leather surface of those tough questions may lie a frightened, aching heart. The mind doubts because the heart fears whether or not we are truly lovable. If the gates to my emotions were thrown open and my hideously huge needs paraded out, what would I do if the love of God turned out to be unreal, or worse, unavailable to me? It seems far safer to keep the iron bars of reasonable doubts firmly in place.

Fear-based paralysis runs rampant through God's people. Our physical disabilities may so humiliate us that we fear risking attempts to do more than that which is safe and comfortable. Addictions retain their hold on us even when we know better. (But what will I do if I can't have a drink when I need one? Or, if I'm not really repulsive because I eat too much, on what will I pin my fears of rejection?) Some cannot give up manipulation because they fear that without their control everything will fall apart. Others just feel helpless in the face of old patterns of living that they cannot change. And some of us have simply built our lives around being ill. We don't know what we would talk about if we ever got better.

Do You Want to Get Well?

To all of these forms of spiritual illness, Jesus raises the question, "Do you want to get well?" For the man at the pool, desiring health and risking the effort to stand were as essential to his healing as Jesus' gift of miraculous power. The voice of fear within him shouted, "No! I don't want to get well. This is the only life I know." Jesus, however, called forth a deeper yearning for wholeness. His command to get up evoked a will to live that was older than the man's fear or illness. So too, Jesus prods even now our desire to live as God's children in radiant light, abundant grace, and flowing health.

"Do you want to get well?" The question echoes beyond our initial negative reply until it reaches to the depths of our spirit which cries, "Yes! Yes I do!"

"Get up. Pick up your mat and walk!" He wasn't very nice

31

about it. In fact, before the man felt ready, Jesus jump-started his faith. Contemporary phrases come to mind for this scene: Get over yourself! Just do it! Get a life! It seems that there comes a time when we simply have to stop thinking about it and rise on wobbly legs, seizing the very pallet of our illness to walk away free of the chronic disease.

Not everyone will be at the same place in their spiritual lives that this man was. I want to be careful to recognize that some forms of illness do not fall away by sheer command. Telling a clinically depressed person to "Buck up!" may do more harm than good. (Telling me that, however, during a mood in which I am particularly stuck in myself may be a big help.) Further, some forms of sickness need to be unraveled slowly and with competent assistance. Perpetrators and victims of abuse don't get better in a moment. Much time and tender, skilled care is needed to draw those poisons out of a person. And while some people are healed of physical impairments by God's grace, other people of similar faith are not. Without Jesus' own knowledge and skill, we would be merely cruel to command the disabled ones to just get up.

We cannot say to others that their illnesses and disabilities are their own faults. There is not an ironclad connection between sickness and sin. Every paralysis does not mean failure of will. Of course not.

But we can begin to probe our own souls as we explore this story. Are there areas in our lives where we have been long paralyzed, to the point that we actually rely on being "invalids" as we make our way through life? Might Jesus' question, "Do you want to be made well?" be particularly poignant for us? His command might be just what we need to get going again.

For the chronic doubter, Jesus' command may mean deciding to live for six months *as if* you fully believed in Christianity, opening yourself to all God might have for you. The devotional anemic may buy a kitchen timer and set it for twenty minutes of prayer a day. All the while, she or he will have to trust God with the prayer, "All right, I'm listening. Wherever you send me, I will go!" Chances are, it won't be very far. And someone else may simply have to phone the pastor *today* and volunteer for the job at the shelter.

More introspectively, one of us might hear Jesus' command just before giving in to the same old anger with the children. "Get up. Don't make an issue of this. You know it isn't important. Take up your pallet and walk." Another might hear the command just before purging the meal eaten with guilt. "Get up. You don't have to do that anymore. Take up your pallet and walk." And another may hear it even as the temptation to sink into a moody sullenness settles for the night. "Get up. This is not your life anymore. Take up your *mood* and walk."

See, You Are Well

When the man made his way to the temple, I imagine he wondered what to do with himself next. He had lived thirty-eight years as an invalid and knew little of how to live as a whole, healthy adult. It would have been tempting to desire the comfortable misery of his old paralysis. That nasty mat may yet have had a beckoning feel of familiarity. His healing came quickly, and then he was separated from Jesus. He was up and walking but needed more, especially since the Pharisees were ready to chastise him for carrying his pallet on the Sabbath.

How blessed he was that Jesus found him in the temple and gave him a bit more instruction. "See, you are well. Sin no more, lest something worse befall you." Jesus knew the danger of falling back into the old ways. While we cannot always make a connection between sin and illness, it seems that in this context the man's sin was to see himself as helpless and to blame others for not getting him to the pool for healing. Jesus wanted him to take responsibility for his own life. Sinning again meant continuing to throw blame away from himself. When the man told the Pharisees, "The man who healed me told me to carry my mat," he failed to own his life. Once again, he needed Jesus to jump-start him back to health.

So Jesus gave the man a marvelous gift to carry with him as he discovered how to live with his newfound mobility. "See, you are well." You are healed; you are whole. How wonderful it would be to hear Jesus say that to me, "You're fine. You're on the right track. You *are* well. Just keep living as one who is well."

In this miracle story, the ability of Jesus to heal the man is never in question. The issue revolves around the man's claiming of the healing power and his continued walking in that health. It took faith for him to live with a new image of himself. Instead of being the "Thirty-eight Year Invalid" he became "The Newly Healed."

Our success in taking up our pallet and walking will depend on our faith to embrace Jesus' words *as if they were directed to us:* "See, you are well." Whenever the old life, the life of fear, the life of helplessness calls to us, we may claim his words: "You are well." Yes, I am well. Jesus declares it. I will carry my pallet and not lie on it. His power makes me well continuously. I embrace that power. I invite it to be part of me.

Learning to Walk Again

A Personal Reflection

One week when I had chosen this passage for daily reflection, I also happened to be afflicted with severe back pain. Lying on the floor trying valiantly to do exercises that would relieve the pain, I wondered, *How am I to hear, "Get up and walk" when that's the one thing I can't do right now?*

Of course it had to do with attitude. Suffering can easily make me relish the role of an invalid. My wife will gladly tell you that I am a high-maintenance person. Normally, I can take care of all my little needs by myself. But when I can't get up, no one could possibly think of all my requirements.

I realized during this time on my back that getting up and walking meant foregoing some of the habits I had thought essential. No, I didn't really need that glass of water by the bed. I could live without getting the newspaper. It was all right if I didn't make the coffee the night before.

During these days, my children found that I was unable to run around as usual. They were delighted. I couldn't play vigorously with them, but neither was I the usual moving target. They could find me. I realized that "being well" meant being present with them and making peace with all the things I couldn't do. Each moment, however, brought a choice.

Invalidism would have meant not being ill but wallowing in being ill and missing the opportunities for "walking" in life all around me. Using this story in prayer did not seem to get my back better any faster. It did, however, make the days of pain count for something. Despite the discomfort there was joy. I felt especially present with my loved ones and graced by God with this time together. The healing from this story occurred first on the inside;

being well while on my back seemed a more than sufficient grace. "Get up and walk" found its way to a tablet on my heart.

Writing on the Heart

We have delved into the feelings of the man who lay as an invalid for thirty-eight years. And we have seen various ways in which his situation appears in contemporary life. Hopefully, we have heard Jesus' words, "Rise, take up your pallet and walk," and "See, you are well" as words that are meaningful to us. Now we are ready to write these words more deeply on our hearts.

Shortly, I will be inviting you to pray in the Eastern Orthodox style of linking your life to the life of the biblical character. The more we pour our feelings into such words, the more we will connect with the story. As we pray, we remain mindful of all the thoughts, feelings, questions, and applications we have gleaned from the story so far. These provide texture to the words of the prayer and make it personal to each one.

I hope you will use this prayer several times. You may want to pray it aloud, varying the tone and loudness of your voice with each praying. The goal is to experience the mystical link between what happened once long ago and the present moment in which the Bible story still brings us the presence of Christ through the story. The watchwords for such a prayer are "As thou wert present there, so likewise be thou present here."[1]

Next, I will invite you to recite a prayer in the style of "St. Patrick's Breastplate," as translated by Mrs. C. F. Alexander.[2] In it, we will bind, or fasten on, Christ's words to the man by the pool as if they were addressed to us. The style is that of invocation—a calling forth. In such prayer, we exercise the uniquely human power to call forth the presence of God with our wills and voices. I think you will be surprised at how powerful such simple invocation can be in your life. The more we bind Christ's words to ourselves, the more indelibly they will be written on our hearts.

Then, I will invite you again to look at an emblem from this story. Notice the location in a particular spot in the world and the words spoken in that unique time. Then feel as well how that unique moment has an eternal quality that reaches you through the symbol. Receive it as a precious gift. Look at the emblem long enough that you can recall it in your mind when the book is closed. In this way, you will have an image of the story to fill your heart during the night or in quiet moments of your day.

Notes

[1] *Service Book of the Holy Orthodox-Catholic Apostolic Church*, translated by Isabel Florence Hapgood (Englewood, NJ: Antiochian Orthodox Christian Archdiocese, 1975), 295.

[2] A portion of this prayer may be found in the Appendix.

Prayers of Identification

The Eastern Orthodox tradition skillfully links identification with characters in the Bible to the present-day worshiper. Such prayers are careful to give the scriptural stories their full integrity as events that occurred once and for all in space and time. Simultaneously, the Orthodox recognize that in the mystery of the "communion of saints" these characters are still available to us as friends and guides. Our lives are shaped by theirs. A revealing phrase from that style of worship states:

As thou wert present there, so likewise be thou present here.

I invite you to pray with the man by the Pool of Bethesda, linking your life to his. Though you begin with the words provided, I hope your own prayers will follow.

O Lord, as you did not allow
The invalid of thirty-eight years
To remain on his pallet,

So bid me rise, even when I do not know
If I want to get up or can.

As you did not hear his excuse
That there were none to help him,
So do not hear me ascribe my weakness
To the fault of another.

Bid me walk, even when I would prefer
The paralysis of habits and helplessness.

Lord Christ, as you reminded
The newly healed of his health,
So declare me well, again and again,
For I long to hear your voice of love.

Remind me sharply to sin no more,
For it would be worse, oh worse,
To return to the pallet of old ways
Now that I have tasted your life.

As you did then, so do now.
Change my name from the
Invalid of Thirty-Eight Years
To the Newly Healed.

Amen.

Prayers of Binding

The ancient prayer of St. Patrick, as translated by Mrs. C. F. Alexander, begins with the phrase, "I bind unto myself today." The one who prays goes on to bind, or fasten on, to his or her life events from Christ's life, the virtues of God's good creation, and the abiding presence of the Spirit. These powers then stand between the worshiper and the forces of evil in the world. In the spirit of that prayer, we too may tie the words of Christ to ourselves. Much as we would buckle on our belts or clasp a necklace, we may fasten on Jesus' words.

St. Patrick's prayer, typical of prayers in the Celtic tradition, is rendered with a pleasant rhythm and a simple rhyme scheme. This makes it easy to remember. The phrases are all succinct. I have attempted to provide an example of a binding prayer in the style of Mrs. Alexander's translation. I invite you to pray it several times each day, to carry it with you, perhaps even to learn it, as a way of fastening Christ's words from this story to yourself. Once again, I hope that your own prayers will grow from using these.

> I bind unto myself the talk
> Of Christ with him for years still lame.
> "Get up! Now take your mat and walk,
> In me made whole, the end of blame."

An Emblem for Faith

On the next page is a symbolic emblem that was created after reflection upon this story. I invite you to spend several moments meditating upon it. Consider the location of the event in a definite, real place. This scene really occurred! Ponder the words of scripture chosen from the story. Consider how they communicate something central about the event, and how they give meaning to life today. Reflect upon how the story is rendered through the art. Allow the emblem to carry the story's meaning to you.

See, you are well again

Jerusalem: The Temple

Three

✦

Taken at Dawn

For in ev'rything
Thy words do find me out, and parallels bring,
And in another make me understood.

George Herbert, "The Holy Scriptures (2)"

The story of the Woman Caught in Adultery is found in John 7:53–8:11.

I stood in the ring of condemnation. The circle was drawn tight by the crowding people who gawked and jeered at me. I could feel them pressing, but they did not come any closer than about ten feet. Instinctively, it seemed, they held their distance from me. Perhaps they thought I would contaminate them. But their emotions surged past any boundaries and splattered all over me. They were furious! How could I have made them this angry?

I wondered how long this would go on. I tried to close out their faces, their shouts, the very waves of hostility that rolled from the sea of their rage. Shutting my eyes, I thought about the hours just past.

He had come to me late last night, after the city was asleep.

I don't know how he managed to leave his home without waking the children. Perhaps he said he needed to check on the animals and thought he would be back after they had returned to sleep and before they woke for the day. He knocked quietly on my door and without even lighting a lamp, I quickly opened it; and he slipped in.

Of course I knew it was not right for him to be there. I also knew that it was not right when he wasn't there. Still, it was a sin. I was a widow, but he had a wife and children. There was no excuse. Loneliness seldom asks for a reason. The rest of my days were so hard—a single woman with no family, trying to live. Yes, it was wrong, except that when he was in my arms it all seemed right. Only in his arms did my life seem bearable. We were torn, both of us, between right and right, wrong and wrong.

And I had reached the point where I didn't care. How much harder could life be? If only I had known. He took more and more risks. I didn't try to stop him. Last night we fell asleep together, and this time neither of us woke before dawn.

We did not stir before the pounding and the shouting. I was sleeping so deeply, lost in the contentment of believing there was no universe beyond that room. How quickly the reality of the world's harsh light flared in my eyes! They came through the door with their torches and their shouts.

I felt as naked as I was. My heart sank into my stomach. Caught! Caught in the act. Everything known. It was all over. The music had stopped. And now I was a pawn in the hands of these self-righteous, holy people.

My love looked as surprised as I. I still believe he had no idea they were coming. There was no time even for a farewell.

They pulled us apart. Someone wrapped my robe roughly around me. "Cover up the tramp! It's a disgrace to look at her!"

Instantly I knew what was up. I had seen it before. The adulterer dragged before the council by a crowd. The reading of the law, the verdict, the stoning.

I expected nothing less. I was frightened. And yet I wasn't. After the initial panic, I didn't care. It just didn't matter. We knew the risks. We had wagered our lives on a few moments of tenderness once a month. For a while we had won. The hour of warmth made the guilt endurable. And now we were caught, and we would die. Life alone was death anyway.

But I hadn't counted on the terrible hatred. It felt as sharp as the stones in their hands.

I thought they would take me to the council. Though it was early, the Pharisees and teachers who led the crowd would have wakened them right away. But instead they brought me to the outer courts of the temple. There was already a crowd assembled, but it wasn't for me. They were listening to a teacher. And that is where I was taken. Rough hands threw me down in the dust before the feet of Jesus, the fanatic prophet from the northlands. He didn't have much of a reputation for going easy on people. That's how I got to this place.

My ears came back into tune. The leaders of the mob were saying something to him. This whole scene seemed to be as much about him as me. "Teacher, we caught this woman in the act of adultery. She cannot deny it."

I don't deny it, you pompous fool. Looking at you makes me proud to have been with him. Of course I don't deny it. Those were my thoughts, but I said nothing aloud.

"Teacher," his voice was full of contempt, "the law says we

should stone such a tramp. What do you say?" The law said that both the man and the woman should be put to death. I wondered why they had only taken me. But this injustice would hopefully mean that my love's life would be spared. I wondered whose fate would be worse.

Then there was silence. Jesus had said nothing in reply. Was he dumbfounded? He seemed to be catching all their anger and absorbing it. For those moments, their rage was deflected from me. It seemed easier to breathe. Silently their venom flowed into him, but he remained still, and they grew quiet. He stooped down near me and wrote something in the dirt.

What did he write? I couldn't see. But it slowed them down. He was not overpowered by their anger. He did not get frenzied. He grew more still.

But they were not satisfied. They pressed him some more. "How about it, teacher? The law says to kill her. What do you say? Are you just? Are you merciful? Lead us!"

I forgot myself for a moment as I grew fascinated by the drama unfolding before me. Jesus had angered a lot of powerful people, both religious and worldly. They knew his reputation as a healer. He had broken the law to heal people on the Sabbath. They knew his reputation as one zealous for holiness. Jesus had overturned the moneychanging tables in the temple, causing huge losses for the local businessmen. But his righteousness was not of the pristine, picky type. He had consistently angered the Pharisees, the party of meticulous law observers. Once he had even changed the water used for ritual cleansing into wine for a wedding feast! That set them off. But none of it had been enough to arrest him.

Now they were trying to catch him conclusively. If he didn't recommend following the law, he could be dismissed once and for all as a law breaker. But if he pressed for the law, he would have set himself against Rome, for they did not allow the Jews to enact the death penalty. Even more, his reputation among the poor and the sick and the sinful would be shattered. He would have sided with the authorities and proved himself to be just another religious entrepreneur who traded on the needs of the broken.

All this went through my mind as the minutes unfolded so slowly—until I remembered with a start that they were talking about me! This was my life in the balance. He was so quiet. Oh, go on and uphold the law, I thought. Let's be done with this. Don't get yourself killed for me. I deserve this, and I knew that when I did it, and I didn't care. I don't care now. I have nothing to live for. Jesus, just give me to them, and you live to confound them another day.

Then he stood up. They went quiet again. He was ready to answer. The life in me rose up. I did care. My heart pounded. Would this be the judgment?

"The one of you who is sinless shall go first. Cast a stone at her." He said it slowly. He looked their anger dead in the face. His words echoed. The one of you who is sinless . . . go first . . . cast a stone at her. Then he stooped down again and wrote on the ground.

I didn't breathe. Silence settled on the circle. Slowly, the tension left the crowd; they seemed to get smaller before my eyes. It looked like the fight went out of them. One of the old men, a scribe, who had been so angry, dropped his arms to his side and turned and walked away. Then another and another.

In five minutes, the crowd was gone and I was left with him. "Woman, where are they? Has no one condemned you?"

I looked around. The death verdict had never come. Nothing more had been said. "No one, sir."

"Neither do I condemn you. Go, and from now on sin no longer." Then he turned away and walked over to a group of men who were waiting for him.

I stood alone in the empty ring. The words he wrote were still in the dirt, though the road dust was quietly eroding the letters. I realized then how disheveled I must have looked. So I put my robe on properly, patted down my hair, and covered my head. I should have started for home, but I couldn't get my feet moving.

"Neither do I condemn you." The words sounded in my head again. No condemnation. I felt it. And only then did I realize how long I had lived under judgment.

When my husband died, a tiny accusation began to grow amidst the grief. Somehow, some way, it had been my fault. I was unworthy of him, and it caused him to get sick and die. I deserved that.

The seed was watered by the way everyone changed toward me. They didn't know what to do with me. We hadn't had any children yet, so the mothers had nothing to talk about with me. It seemed I was deficient. The other widows were all older. They looked at me with suspicion, as if I were a widow because I wanted to be, as if I hadn't earned a place of respect. I was still pretty, and they seemed to hate me for that. My youth and my appearance were that of a virgin, but I was not. I was damaged goods, waiting to ruin another man.

And that is exactly what I had done, though I never set out to do that. I gave in to the loneliness. I became what I was accused of being. And no one could have condemned me as much as I did myself. Oh, I thought about his wife and children every second that we were not together. For every day but one a month when we met, I lived under the sentence of death. I condemned myself, but I could not stop myself. I was a prisoner.

So it was almost a relief to have been caught, except that my accusers were just so stupid. They actually thought I liked my life, that I somehow relished sin, that I was somehow different than they were. Even in the circle of their condemnation, I was not known or understood. And that too seemed to be my fault.

Until he spoke to them. "The one of you who is sinless shall go first. Cast a stone at her." And they could not. For they were just like me. Jesus linked me again to other people. They understood then that we were not so different. Each has fallen to weakness. No one is worthy to pick up the stone.

That alone, though, would have been small consolation. I already knew how awful I was. It was not such a comfort for me to see that everyone else felt the same way. But then he set me free.

Quietly, simply, he had said, "Neither do I condemn you." For he could have, and I would have been glad. He alone seemed capable of passing judgment. And he let me go. No condemnation. All the angry voices, within and without, were silenced. No condemnation. I was clean.

It felt as if the crowd really had thrown their stones, and that I had died but now lived again. Life was new. The world was open before me.

"Go your way and sin no more." That was a given. I would never speak to the man who had been my lover for the last year again. I knew this as a matter of fact. I felt the loss of him, but with the same kind of pain that I had when I finally accepted my husband's death. This is the way life is. There is pain, but still there is life. I was to go my way now, wherever that might be.

That terrible growth of accusation had been scooped out from within me. There was room now for something else to grow within. While life arose in me, the vacant space in my soul seemed to be guarded by his words, "Neither do I condemn you." That sentence would nurture the new life in me.

I felt sure of that as I started for home, though I didn't have any idea what I would be doing next. And that was all right. For there were no more accusations. The circle of condemnation had become a ring of grace.

Praying with the Woman Caught in Adultery

As we continue to invite scripture to shape our lives, we continue to pray from the perspective of the Bible characters, in order that our identification with them might deepen. Try on these prayers as if they were your own, as if you were the woman caught in adultery. And then, I hope you will be moved to compose your own prayers in concert with this woman who encountered the grace of Christ.

I

Great God, their eyes upon me
Are worse than your all-seeing gaze!

Taken at Dawn

They have demanded this exposure;
They rip my arms away from love,
Tearing my clothes to leer and curse.
I am caught and naked to them
As I am to you.

Do you like what you see?
I do not.

I know my sin; it is ever before me.
But did that stop me?

No, I had to be caught.
And by these fools.

For you know that I was sealed
Away, deaf and blind in heart.

I was numb.

Only the moments of sin
Made me feel alive, but each one
Deadened me more.

Until you sent these honchos
To yank me from bed,
I was lost in loathing myself.

Now I feel your eyes upon me

In their stares.
I await your judgment with relief.

II

My heart grows as quiet
As the crowd when you speak.

They look at you and not at me.
They turn away; not one
Will cast the stone.

And then you look at me,
But your eyes do not burn.
You see all; I cannot hide
But now want to be found.

"Neither do I condemn."

Neither do I condemn.
The words trickle through me
Like water through cracks
Finding every space beneath
The surface, washing away
Old dirt.

Neither do I condemn.
You still the voices
Without and within.
I stand in the first

Peaceful silence I have heard
In years.
I will go my way, then,
As you have said and
Sin no more.
Neither do I condemn
Myself
Thanks to you.

An Emblem for Faith

On the next page is a symbolic emblem that was created after reflection upon this story. I invite you to spend several moments meditating upon it. Consider the location of the event in a definite, real place. Ponder the words of scripture chosen from the story. Consider how they communicate something central about the event, and how they give meaning to life today. Reflect upon how the story is rendered through the art. Allow the emblem to carry the story's meaning to you.

Neither do I condemn you

Jerusalem: The Temple Courts

Four

Neither Do I Condemn You

Heav'n lies flat in thee,
Subject to ev'ry mounter's bended knee.

George Herbert, "The Holy Scriptures (I)"

From childhood we know the awful feeling of being caught right in the middle of disobedience. The coins stolen from my mother's purse clanked unmistakably as I walked up the stairs toward her. The forbidden ice cream spilled all over the floor as if in conspiracy with my parents. I could never get it cleaned up before they entered the room. And of course the door always squeaked the loudest when I tried to sneak back home after midnight.

To be caught is to be exposed with no possibility for escape or denial. The bottom falls out. There is a hollow feeling in the stomach. Our breath catches and skin prickles. Faces flush. The mind cries out "Oh no!" Fear and shame may turn to anger and then to blame of others, but all protestations are ultimately useless. We are nailed, as in T. S. Eliot's phrase, "pinned and wriggling on the wall."

As adults we hear such exposure in different words but with no less humiliating effect. My wandering mind may be jerked back from distraction with the words of a child, "You never listen to me." The insightful parishioner may finally say, "Preacher, you use prayer as a cover for not dealing with my feelings." Or the personnel review may reveal the very weakness I have struggled so hard to cover.

Who can endure the accusations that name us so precisely? They seem to reel off the page of some nightmare list of charges:

"You told me that you quit, but I know you drank too much last night."

"You really aren't doing this for me at all; you're thinking only of yourself."

"He's not really divorced yet, but she sees him anyway!"

"You use your religion as a cover to get out of the house."

"This work was never done with any intention of being a good job. You faked it."

And, as if present condemnation weren't enough, far too many of us live with accusations from years ago. Most of them are not even based on fact. But still they fly at us:

"This was done to me because secretly I wanted it."

"If you ever tell anyone, I'll kill you."

"Daddy left because of me."

"I do not deserve anything more than this."

"Can't you do anything right?"

"You're so ugly; no one will ever want you."

"How can you be so dumb? Are you just plain stupid, son?"

The voices replay in our hearts and minds, often when we are not even conscious of them. And we live out the commands with an exacting, destructive obedience. Then we find ourselves in the ring of judgment, surrounded by those who are ready to throw their stones.

The woman in our story was trapped in such a circle. She was without excuse, literally caught in the act. But she is not beyond understanding. In the expanded narrative, I speculated that she entered an adulterous relationship with a man partly because she had internalized the fear and projections of others upon her. She became what they expected her to be. Her very isolation caused her to cease to respect the forms and codes of those who live in community. Ostracized by the enforcers of the rules, she tried to live outside them. This is an understandable reaction, which, as we too painfully know from experience, never quite works.

The Judging Crowd

While we readily identify with this woman in her shame, we may also identify with her accusers. Self-righteous anger grows like summer weeds in human souls. We seem to relish the opportunity to make an airtight case against someone. It is all too delightful to sum up another's life in terms of their sin and then pass our sentence.

These days, many of us have heard enough basic psychology to know something about projection. That which we dislike in ourselves we project onto others. So those things that make me angriest about someone are probably the very things I fear discovering in myself. This helps to explain why a seemingly insignificant act can push our hot buttons and send us into rages far beyond any reasonable response.

Thanks to M. Scott Peck's book *People of the Lie* we know too that evil is most clearly defined as the inability to admit fault. The refusal to own our sinfulness causes us to act with all manner of ugliness toward others. You have probably seen this enacted in those people who are never wrong. Nothing that has ever happened to them has ever been their fault. Someone else is always responsible. We look at him or her and stand amazed that so many things could "just happen" to one person. All personal responsibility for life has been thrown onto someone else.

Of course, knowing all this about the way people work has not stopped us from placing people into the ring of accusation. When there is a chance for a good stoning of someone caught in the act, our hands may all too readily twitch in anticipation as they grip the rocks. We're ready to hurl them. We've got so much pent-up anger at the way the world is that we can't wait to let it fly. We may blush to discover how thrilled we are to find someone who so richly deserves our judgment.

Blame is easy. We love to shift the guilt, to put the whole load somewhere else. After all, our own guilty bags are so heavy that we don't need any more.

Writing in the Dirt

The story never tells us what Jesus wrote when he bent near the ground. This enigmatic line has kept readers speculating for years. Perhaps Jesus was writing Bible verses related to the incident. Or maybe he was writing the sins and names of those who accused the woman. Perhaps he scribbled a message of hope to her, or maybe he was just doodling. In any event, the effect of his kneeling to write was a change in the very energy of the moment.

Self-righteous anger is intense and wants expression immediately. When my case seems airtight, I am ready to go to war for it, right now. I can hear myself steaming, "Why, if only that so and so were here now, I'd really give him a piece of my mind." In those moments before the angry mob, there were waves of urgent energy demanding that Jesus decide quickly. A lesser person could easily have been swept up in the intensity.

But by writing on the ground, Jesus derailed the train of accusation. First, he shifted the focus from the woman to himself. Then, he refused to be drawn into their timetable. Finally, he shifted the focus back to the accusers.

He forced the situation to "count to a hundred," to breathe, to slow down. Then he said slowly, "Those of you who are sinless be the first to cast a stone at her" (translation mine). He called for the stoning as an expression of righteous anger on the one justly accused. But he qualified it first. You sinless ones. Who fit the category?

Then Jesus broke the rhythm of the moment again by stooping to write. He forced them to think. They would now have to make a judgment about themselves. He didn't call for those who had not committed this crime, but rather for those who had committed no sin, ever. His words and actions were powerful enough to cause the accusers to look inward and recognize their sin. Jesus broke the power of evil, which does not admit fault; and so he opened the way for compassion.

We may build a case that seems airtight against someone. Our condemnation appears flawless and moves toward expression in a blast of anger. When we feel that right and are so certain that someone else is that wrong, we can be fairly sure that we have not heard Jesus' words. We remain under judgment. We are ripe for him to ask, "Are you sinless?" The return on our unexamined accusation is judgment back upon us. If we are not stopped before we throw the stones, if this projection is not recognized, then the terrible damage will be done to another person and to ourselves. The shame from our fury will be buried and turn into more fury, more unresolvable grudges, more separation.

By contrast, the humiliation of walking away from the woman left her former accusers open to receive the compassion of Jesus. With self-righteous judgment broken, they were in line for grace. He caused them to move into her position through self-examination. So the perpetrators joined the victim in the circle, and Jesus alone was left to dispense punishment or grace.

Where Are Your Accusers?

Jesus took up the position that only the sinless one was in a position to judge, and only God (through Jesus) is sinless. He silenced the voices of all the woman's prosecutors. And he silenced the accusations within. "Where are your accusers?" he asked. "Has no one condemned you?" She replied that no one had. "Then neither do I condemn you. Go and sin no more."

Jesus communicated to the woman that the only voice she needed to listen to was the voice of God, and that voice did not ring out in condemnation but in forgiveness. There were no excuses for her sin; it remained wrong and off limits. But the cycle of shame and judgment was broken.

Jesus willingly brought the righteous accusers into awareness that they too deserved condemnation. Then, from such a point of humility, they would be as ready as the woman to hear the words, "Neither do I condemn you; go and sin no more."

Writing on the Heart

Psalm 51 is a deeply felt prayer of confession that includes, "The sacrifices of God are a broken spirit; a broken and contrite heart, O God, you will not despise" (Psalm 51:17, NIV). From a position of weakness, we are open to grace. When we stop projecting our guilt through blame of others, we are ready to hear that "there is now no condemnation for those who are in Christ Jesus" (Rom. 8:1, NIV).

Being caught takes the breath away and creates a hollow place of shame. We may try to fill the void with buckets of accusations for others. But that only deepens our shame. Instead, if we will receive, Jesus offers to pour his own grace into that vacuum.

As we prepare to write this story on our hearts, I invite you to imagine those places in which you would love to hear Jesus say, "Neither do I condemn you." Your reflections might be these:

- For the marriage you entered into when you were too young to know what you were doing, which ended in a divorce that seemed the only alternative. The pain of it continues to this day.
- For words spoken to your children, for anger that you passed on to them when you should have dealt with it in another way, for all the blame you unjustly gave them, and for your worries now about their lives which are so far from yours.

- For actions of greed when you were out of control with your finances and the desire of your eyes.
- For betrayals of friends and spouse, of confidences and knowledge, the consequences of which you are still reaping.
- For the aging parent whom you neglected during the long years of illness, while your brother or sister provided all the care. You just couldn't bear to go.
- For failures of courage, wasted time, and unrealized goals.

For these and so many others, hear Jesus' words, "Neither do I condemn you. Go and sin no more."

Neither Do I Condemn You

Prayers of Identification

The Eastern Orthodox tradition skillfully links identification with characters in the Bible to the present-day worshiper. Such prayers are careful to give the scriptural stories their full integrity as events that occurred once and for all in space and time. Simultaneously, the Orthodox recognize that in the mystery of the "communion of saints" these characters are still available to us as friends and guides. Our lives are shaped by theirs. A revealing phrase from that style of worship states:

As thou wert present there, so likewise be thou present here.

I invite you to pray with the woman caught in adultery, linking your life to hers. Though you begin with the words provided, I hope your own prayers will follow.

O Jesus, you did not allow the rage of accusers
To carry the day against the woman caught,
So do not, I pray, allow my self-righteous fits to
Bring condemnation before compassion.

Ever drive me to examine myself before I speak,
Before I act in anger and rage.
Great Lord, command me to drop the stones.

Lord Jesus, you stood with the woman
In the circle of hate
And guarded her with your presence and your words,
So guard me against those voices, within and without

Which wreak judgment upon me,
Though I know too well that I am deserving of stones.

Protect me with your words,
"Neither do I condemn"
That there may be a quiet place in me
Where your grace will flourish.

Prayers of Binding

The ancient prayer of St. Patrick, as translated by Mrs. C. F. Alexander, begins with the phrase, "I bind unto myself today." The one who prays goes on to bind, or fasten on, to his or her life events from Christ's life, the virtues of God's good creation, and the abiding presence of the Spirit. These powers then stand between the worshiper and the forces of evil in the world. In the spirit of that prayer, we too may tie the words of Christ to ourselves. Much as we would buckle on our belts or clasp a necklace, we may fasten on Jesus' words.

St. Patrick's prayer, typical of prayers in the Celtic tradition, is rendered with a pleasant rhythm and a simple rhyme scheme. This makes it easy to remember. The phrases are all succinct. I have attempted to provide an example of a binding prayer in the style of Mrs. Alexander's translation. I invite you to pray it several times each day, to carry it with you, and perhaps even to learn it, as a way of fastening Christ's words from this story to yourself. Once again, I hope that your own prayers will grow from using these.

I fasten to myself this hour
Christ's kneeling on the ground to write

The words which stopped their anger's power:
"If you've no sin, then hurl your spite!"

I bind to me our Lord who stayed
By her whose sin deserved the stone,
Till each accuser turned away,
"Nor do I condemn, you leave atoned."

I bind unto myself this shift,
From righteous judge to heart revealed,
From critic widening every rift,
To child in Jesus' grace concealed.

An Emblem for Faith

On the next page is a symbolic emblem that was created after reflection upon this story. I invite you to spend several moments meditating upon it. Consider the location of the event in a definite, real place. This scene really occurred! Ponder the words of scripture chosen from the story. Consider how they communicate something central about the event, and how they give meaning to life today. Reflect upon how the story is rendered through the art. Allow the emblem to carry the story's meaning to you.

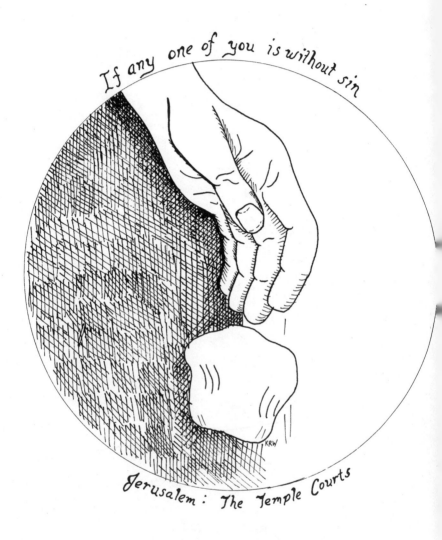

If any one of you is without sin

Jerusalem: The Temple Courts

Five

❧❦❧

Two Sisters and
Their Loss

O Book! infinite sweetness! let my heart
Suck ev'ry letter, and a honey gain.

George Herbert "The Holy Scriptures (I)"

The story of Lazarus, Martha, and Mary is found in John 11:1-44.

Martha's Story

How we adored our brother! All my life I have thought of
Lazarus as my protector. He was a constant source of security.
Since we were children, Lazarus tried to look after my sister,
Mary, and me. Of course there were many times when I didn't
think he was nearly as smart and brave as he thought he was! In
the early years, he tried to lord it over us quite a lot. But we always found ways around his bossiness. We knew that underneath
the surface his love burned brightly for us. And as the years

passed away, along with our parents, his interest in us grew gentler. We all became friends. Our "family" worked beautifully.

We were content as a threesome. None of us was married, but we all looked after one another. Because we were siblings, there were none of the usual barriers caused by the fixed roles between husband and wife. Lazarus knew better than to try to exclude us from decisions! No taboos forbade our frank exchanges. We had nothing to withhold from him and nothing to fear. Each trusted the other, and so each of us had a role in keeping the household together.

Lazarus maintained our place in the community. As a man, he could trade for goods in the market and contribute to the decisions of the leaders. He made his two unmarried sisters legitimate in the eyes of the world. His standing in Bethany was conferred upon us. So Lazarus was our security and our link to the world.

My work was to keep order in the home. I was always concerned to see that everyone was in the right place at the right time. I knew quite a bit about the responsibilities my brother had, and I tried to help him fulfill his obligations. During the growing season, I reminded Lazarus when he needed to check on the fields. Or if he had to meet one of the other men from town, I saw that he got there well prepared.

To me, our house was our haven. It had to be neat. The chores must never be neglected. Water must be clean and available; the fire should always be bright and warm. Above all, the table must always be full. No one in my home would ever go hungry. Seeing that everyone was well fed made me content. Only if they were comfortable could I be at ease. I made sure that Lazarus and Mary felt that home was a source of nurture. I loved to take care of them.

Mary's work is more difficult to describe. Naturally, she helped me fetch water or sweep the floor, but those jobs never truly interested her. If I hadn't stayed after her, she would never have completed any of her jobs! I think that Mary's gift was to bring a sense of life to all of us. She lived to be with people. It didn't matter to her what the house looked like or when we ate, as long as she could be talking to someone. Guests loved to come to our home because of Mary. She was the life in the family.

While I thought of people's needs for hospitality, Mary thought of their feelings. I could feed the body to contentment. Mary touched everyone's heart. Sometimes I was jealous of her knack with people. But mostly I was like everyone else. I just enjoyed being with her. I think that it was mainly because of Mary that Jesus had become so close to us.

We met him at a wedding feast; and we were each, in our own way, quite taken with him. Soon after, we invited him to dinner. He left his disciples and came alone. Our three-person family seemed to be just what he needed. Jesus had always treated women with more respect than other men did. So I think he liked the openness in our household. He willingly entered the give-and-take of our discussions.

That night, I tried my best to make the house seem like a place of welcome. I wanted him to take his ease with us. The meal was my specialty, and I beamed to see him eat as if he truly enjoyed it. Later he mentioned how pleasant it was to be hosted with no burning questions asked, no ill relatives to be healed, and nothing more required of him than his presence. He couldn't have said anything kinder in the world to someone like me!

Jesus and Lazarus got along like old friends from the first night. Lazarus wasn't like Jesus' twelve disciples. He was, if I may brag as a sister, more understanding than they. Lazarus had a place among the leaders in town, but, like Jesus, he gave blind loyalty to no one's special cause. Lazarus yearned for a different solution to our nation's problems than the rebel cries of the zealots or the untouchable piety of the Pharisees. He knew there had to be another way. Jesus seemed drawn to his openness to a new vision.

My brother loved the scriptures, and he knew them well. The two men talked often about the meaning of different passages. Sometimes they would disagree at first and go back and forth over a point of the law. But Lazarus never argued as an enemy. He didn't mind when Jesus would give him an insight into a meaning he had not imagined before. Lazarus knew that Jesus was no ordinary man. He willingly allowed Jesus to be his mentor. But he learned without the starry-eyed devotion of the crowds that used to follow Jesus. Lazarus engaged the Lord, and Jesus loved him for that.

But as I said, I believe it was Mary who most drew Jesus to us. Her great heart threw its gates open wide whenever she was near Jesus. Mary's love of life seemed to recognize immediately that Jesus embodied life itself. He was vivid, shimmering with energy. Mary used to say that she could feel the intimacy Jesus had with God. He called the Lord "Father" in a way that hinted of personal experience. Mary was completely devoted to him. She wanted to be near him every minute. But she did not cling to him like the needy crowds. Rather, she approached Jesus with all her joy awakened. She recognized that Jesus himself was the satisfaction of her yearnings.

Jesus always looked at each of us with kind compassion in his eyes. He understood, and his gaze seemed to reach places no one had ever seen before. But when he looked at Mary, there was something more. His face went softer, sometimes sadder. He looked as if he were handling something very precious and very fragile. Mary's open devotion touched him deeply. Most people loved Jesus because they wanted something from him, and he gave it. Mary simply wanted to give him her heart. It would be enough for her if he would receive her ardor. And he did. I wonder if he didn't seem so sad around her sometimes because he knew that such great hearts, like his own, are prone to being broken.

We knew Jesus for nearly three years. There were not many visits, because Jesus spent most of his time north of us in Galilee. But each visit was precious. We felt as if we helped him along his difficult way. And he certainly became the most important person in the life of our family. We hosted him when we could. The rest of the time we went about our business, but we always listened for any news about what he was doing. We were so proud to be his friends.

An Interruption

Life seemed so blessed in those days that we were taken completely by surprise when Lazarus became ill. At first it just seemed like a winter chill. Others in the village had been sick and soon recovered. But as the days passed, Lazarus grew weaker. His fever worsened.

I did everything I knew how to do to get him better. I made

him his favorite soup, but he hardly touched it. I wiped his brow with cold cloths, but they only gave him chills. So I brought him warm ones, but they made him feel like he was burning up. Medicines did nothing.

A sense of panic began to overtake me. I just wanted to do something to help my brother. Somehow, I should have been able to fix things. I doubted myself. Why couldn't I do enough? Why did nothing I tried seem to help?

All that time, Mary hovered close by. She held her brother's hand and spoke gently to him. He seemed to like to have her close. When he slept, Mary stayed by and prayed silently. But she was too upset to be of much use to me. A number of times I wished that she could just once warm a cloth for me or go to fetch fresh water. It was hard doing all the work alone. But she wouldn't leave Lazarus, and I guess that was her part.

After a few days I realized the awful truth. Lazarus was dying. Nothing I could do would fix things. It became very clear that there was only one solution. Jesus could make him well. We had prided ourselves on not being like all the others who came to Jesus with their needs. But now there was no choice. I knew that Jesus had crossed the Jordan to the place where John had conducted his baptisms. It was about a two-day journey. Praying that we hadn't waited too long, I sent messengers to Jesus.

The hours crept by. Lazarus grew weaker. Would the messengers get there in time? If my brother could just hang on for four days, Jesus would have time to get here, and he would make everything all right.

But Jesus didn't come. And Lazarus died two days after we sent the messengers. Still, I held out some hope. We believed that the spirit of a dead person stayed near the body for three days after death. Lazarus could still be revived, just as the daughter of Jairus had been.

We wrapped the body in the preserving spices of aloe and myrrh, then bound the body in soft, clean grave clothes. We laid his body inside the family tomb. Oh, who would have thought we would need it so soon! A great stone was rolled against the opening.

There was no sign of Jesus. Still I held out hope that he would come in time.

Back home, I felt distraught. I should have watched for signs of illness more closely. I should have tended him better or gone and gotten help. I should have sent for Jesus sooner. There were a hundred things I could have done differently.

But shortly, the regrets, the questioning, and the guilt were all lost in a swirl of activity. Dozens of friends and relatives had arrived from Jerusalem to grieve the death and attend the entombment. I was busy then. At last I had a use in the world again. They all had to be fed. Mary was beside herself with grief. So the work fell to me. As I cooked and cleaned and cooked some more, I kept wondering, *What's keeping Jesus?*

The third day since death came and went. There was no hope now. The spirit was gone. I began to wonder how two unmarried sisters were going to get by. There'd be more work for me. I'd just have to learn how to manage the affairs that Lazarus had looked after. I thought all through the night about all the things I would need to know.

Writing on the Heart

"If You Had Been Here..."

The next day, I was still brooding as I worked. While I was preparing supper for the guests, a neighbor came in and told me she had seen Jesus on the road to town. I dropped the pot I was washing and hurried out to meet him.

"Lord, if you had been here, my brother would not have died." I was surprised that those were the first words out of my mouth. I didn't mean to accuse him. But Jesus had been the only one who could have fixed the problem. I didn't mean to imply that he was at any fault. So hardly knowing what I intended, I added quickly, "Yet even now I know that God will grant you whatever you ask."

He looked me full in the face and said, "Your brother will rise again."

I thought I knew what he meant. We were among those Jews who believed in life after death. One day, God will raise all the dead to life. Jesus had meant to comfort me, and I understood. "Yes, Lord, on the day of resurrection, all will live again."

Then he said, "I am the resurrection. And the life. The one who believes in me will live even if he dies. Do you believe this?"

My mind was spinning. But whatever he said, I believed. It all came out of me then. I hoped he wouldn't think it heresy. No one had said this before; we hadn't dared to ask him if it were so. I told him who I thought he was, "Yes, Lord, I believe that you are the Christ, the son of the living God, who was sent into the world."

He seemed to accept what I had said as a matter of course. I hadn't spoken blasphemy to say so much about a mere man. But I also thought that there was something more he wanted me to understand. His attention shifted then, and he said he wanted to see Mary. And so I turned and headed for home. I didn't understand, but my hopes were rising faster than I could think. I needed to get Mary. Perhaps she would grasp what he meant. She could feel the meaning I couldn't name.

She was in the house, surrounded by relatives, grieving. "Mary, the Teacher is here, and he's asking for you. I'll take care of the guests. You go on." Quietly, quickly Mary slipped from the house and headed out toward the road.

Praying with Martha

Before continuing with the story, I invite you to pause and pray with the character of Martha. Allow her prayer to be yours and her experience in this story to be your own:

I

I don't know what to do.
Why don't you come?
I will do whatever you say,
There is no other place to turn.

Lord, I have done everything I can think of to do,
And still he grows weaker.
My brother slips away.

Pots, pans, cloths, blankets,
Fires and pails of water
Have been my refuge,
My very present help in this trouble.

Because you are not here and
You do not even send word.
There are no instructions for
This untimely hour, this illness out of season.

Great God, I go over and over
Every detail in my mind
To see if there is something to change.
Have I caused this? Have I failed?

And I can find nothing of substance
Though I would gladly be shown it.
I hear no clear direction from you
Though I beg for it.

II

Lord, if you had been here,
My brother would not have died.
I do not mean disrespect.
You were the only solution to this problem.
And even now you can make things right.

Your promises of hope are so strange.
They do not fit the way the world works.
The body stinks by now, the spirit is gone.
One day, one day things will be right,
I do not grasp what you intend to do in the present.

76

I know that I cannot shake this faith.
The loss breaks my heart but I cannot
Be rid of you. I do not understand you,
But I·believe you are the Son of God.
I cannot help myself.

Mary's Story

I never knew how much I loved Lazarus until he was gone. He had just always been a part of my life. He was my big brother. Sometimes when we were children, he acted like he didn't have time for his little sisters. But I knew he loved us, and I never let him forget that for too long. Lazarus had never been one who could hide his feelings behind his face. His heart was too honest to allow him to pretend. It wasn't hard to learn how to get him to laugh when he was off on a tirade. Or to tell when he was frightened and to lend him a few encouraging words. I knew Lazarus better than he knew himself.

I couldn't imagine life without him. The three of us were so close. We were a family. We were supposed to be together. So after the funeral, sitting in that room with all the relatives around, I kept falling apart. Lazarus would fill my mind, and I would see him working through a passage of scripture. His face was so earnest as he squinted his eyes into the problem, as if he were working against a strong wind. And then I would hear him laughing. He had the big, jolly laugh of a man whose heart hides no guile. Or I would see him conducting his business in the marketplace, and I felt again how proud I was that this fine, strong man was my brother. And then, as if I hadn't known before, I would realize that he was gone, and I dissolved again into a puddle of grief.

During those days, my heart was a watercourse of tears. It ran along for hours babbling of Lazarus. But often it would split into two, and another stream would run toward Jesus. I missed him. I needed him here to help me understand. From the first time we met, Jesus seemed to know me through and through. He seemed strong enough and kind enough to hold my heart in his hands. I willingly gave it to him. I had never seen anyone so filled with life in all its passion and variety. Jesus had more joy than a gang of children and more grief than this room full of mourners in my house. All at once, Jesus carried the fullness of living, good and bad, painful and bright, within himself. His life called forth every cubit of my own. Just his presence seemed to awaken me.

Jesus had been Lazarus's best friend. Though they saw each other only rarely, the two acted as if they had known each other forever. When Lazarus was so sick, I knew he needed Jesus. I didn't know exactly what Jesus would do for him. But I was sure the two needed to be together. I felt relieved the day Martha told me she had sent for him.

The waiting was terrible. For a while I could lose myself in caring for my brother. I tried to pour all the health I possessed through my hands and into him as I wiped his brow. It didn't work. And then I would cry out inside, "Jesus! Why don't you come? This is Lazarus whom you love, and he is beyond anyone's help but yours. We need your life!"

I kept wondering if it were my fault. If I had been different, if I had loved more, perhaps this wouldn't have happened. If I had been a better person, God might have spared my brother. I just felt like I should have been able to will Lazarus to be connected to the healing source. I should have been able to get Jesus to come there sooner. It was my poor love that failed him.

But the nightmare deepened. Too quickly, Lazarus slipped away from us. I couldn't hold him here. We laid him in the tomb, and four days passed before Jesus arrived.

When Martha told me that Jesus was here and asking for me, the urgency behind all my waiting burst through me. I ran from the room. Relief, anger, sorrow, and questions all clamored for expression. I saw him there on the road, and I was overwhelmed. He was the object of my yearning and my love. I had waited so long; he hadn't been here when I needed him. And then he arrived. I fell down at his feet.

The words came out on their own. "Lord, if you had been here, my brother would not have died!" The whole force of my need was behind that cry. Jesus had to know that he was the only one who could have helped Lazarus. It made such good sense to me: I needed Lazarus; Lazarus needed Jesus; therefore, I needed Jesus. Jesus was essential to the story. And he had been missing. So everything fell apart. But now here he was. Oh, Jesus!

He didn't say anything for a long time. He looked at me, and I could see his face change. He had a look that was reserved just for me, and it passed across his features in that moment. Then his expression changed, first to sadness, then to anger. Not at me. He looked at the family who had followed me out. And he began to breathe quickly. His color changed. The weight of the world seemed to be upon him. Anger, sorrow, longing, love all collided in him. He put his hand on my hair. I could feel him swaying with emotion.

"Where have you laid him?"

"Come and see," they answered. The group started for the

tomb. I got up and walked beside him. Jesus couldn't contain his emotions any longer. He began to cry as he walked. It seemed too much for him. And it scared me. He felt the loss of his friend, I was sure. He felt my emotions as well. As usual, he held my heart in his hands. But there was more than that. Jesus seemed to be crying for all of us, for the whole world, over the death of his friend.

We reached the tomb. Jesus sighed deeply, then found his voice. "Roll away the stone!"

Did he want to look at Lazarus one last time? Did he regret missing the burial? He knew that no one was allowed to disturb the dead. It was unclean. But we had to let him see his friend. Then my sister spoke up. She was thinking more practically than the rest of us.

"But Lord, it has been four days! By now there will be a stench!" Oh, bless Martha for thinking of that!

Jesus answered her, "Did I not tell you that if you believed you would see the glory of God?" He motioned, and the stone was rolled away. Martha was right. The odor was terrible.

But Jesus seemed not to notice. He lifted his face in prayer. Then he cried out in a loud voice, "Lazarus, come forth!"

What had he said? How could this be? It frightened me, and I fell to the ground again. There was the sound of movement in the tomb. And there stood my brother, wrapped head to toe in grave clothes.

"Unbind him, and let him go!"

No one dared to refuse him, even as frightened as they were. With those words, the great emotions seemed to pass through Jesus and leave him. He relaxed. He seemed to grow smaller as the exhaustion came upon him.

He had been so grieved, so troubled, so filled with passion. And now here was my brother. I forgot Jesus then. The stream of my emotions shifted course once more and turned toward Lazarus. I ran to my brother and clasped him to me. The myrrh and aloe got all over my clothes. His odor was so strange! He seemed confused to be standing in the sunlight. But none of that mattered to me. All that counted was that he was back.

Praying with Mary

As we continue to invite scripture to shape our lives, we continue to pray from the perspective of the Bible characters in order that our identification with them might deepen. Try on these prayers as if they were your own, as if you were Mary who realized that if Jesus had been there her brother Lazarus would not have died. And then I hope you will be moved to compose your own prayers.

O Lord, I cry out for you,
But I can find you nowhere.
The calls of my soul search
Heaven and earth, but you stay hidden.

My brother needs you.
I need you.
Jesus, you have always been so close to us.
Everyone says you love Lazarus.
Why do you delay?

Is it something I did or something I am?

Writing on the Heart

You know my heart is yours.
Shape me any way you want me.
Only come back to us.

No, my faults in devotion are not the cause.
You remain for reasons of your own.

Lord, if you had been here,
My brother would not have died!
I wanted to pierce you with those words
And it frightened me to see that I did.

Oh Jesus, did I add to your grief?
While you were away, I could not imagine
That you cared so much.
Now I see. Now I see that you weep
For Lazarus and for me.

Suddenly, my sorrow seems shallow
As it is swept up in the great waves of your pain.
I did not know. I could not see.
Is this what you live with every moment
While you look at us here,
Struggling blindly along?

Oh Jesus, if you had been here . . .
You were here. You are.

An Emblem for Faith

On the next page is a symbolic emblem that was created after reflection upon this story. I invite you to spend several moments meditating upon it. Consider the location of the event in a definite, real place. Ponder the words of scripture chosen from the story. Consider how they communicate something central about the event, and how they give meaning to life today. Reflect upon how the story is rendered through the art. Allow the emblem to carry the story's meaning to you.

Six

❧❧❧

He Waited and He Wept

Precious for any grief in any part;
To clear the breast, to mollify all pain.

George Herbert, "The Holy Scriptures (I)"

Unlike the man by the pool or the woman caught in adultery, Mary and Martha did not have any particular need when they first met Jesus. They were different than most of the people we meet in the Gospels because of what they were able to give to him. The fact that Jesus "loved" Lazarus and his sisters indicates a kind of peer relationship. Jesus found friends in this family of three grown siblings. They provided him with refreshment for body and soul.

And then life turned suddenly when Lazarus became deathly ill. This was not part of the plan for people who had been healthy and prosperous. They had always been contributors, not takers. But as Lazarus grew worse, they needed the healing of Jesus as much as anyone ever had. This is a story, then, for those of us who have done fairly well most of the time in the business of living. It's for good people who find suddenly that the sadness in life is very indiscriminate in its choosing.

The Gospel of John unfolds the story in a way that intends to produce conflicting feelings in us. We are set up for a shock. "Jesus loved Martha and her sister and Lazarus" (John 11:5, NRSV). If you were casually listening to this story, your mind would already be completing the sentence, "So he went immediately to his friend who was sick and healed him." But what we hear is, "[So] he stayed two days longer in the place where he was (John 11:6, NRSV). The narrative makes us perk up our ears. Why did Jesus delay? Especially, why did he wait when he was needed by a friend?

Faithful Anguish

We are face-to-face with the experience of the absence of God. We believe that God is present with us at all times. Many of us have a sense of that presence ever about us. But there are times when people of every degree of faith feel that they can no longer find God. And this may happen just at the moment when we need God the most.

For example, we may be striving to make a crucial decision that will affect the course of our lives. We pray hourly for guidance. But the heart cries out, "Where are you? Why don't you show me the way? I want to do what you want me to do, but I don't hear from you."

Or we may realize suddenly that we are slipping into the failure of a relationship or a job. As we fall, we scramble for a handhold to save us. We pray; we read scripture; our souls shout. And it feels as if God is standing above, on the edge of the mountain, watching indifferently as we plummet.

Someone very dear to us may be in critical need. We call the prayer chain. We get everyone we see involved in sending thoughts and prayers God's way. We fall to our knees, beg, demand, plead for help. Nothing happens. Something, either in us or in God, is very wrong.

I have speculated that Martha and Mary went through a time when they blamed themselves for Lazarus's death and even for Jesus' delay. Martha worried that she hadn't *done* the right things. She questioned her timing. She doubted her skill. There was a problem to be solved right in front of her, and she could not bring about a solution. Somehow, that had to be her fault.

So we too may blame ourselves for not doing enough when someone is in need. And there are always enough scraps of evidence against us to build a reasonable case. Of course we could have done things differently. Nobody ever feels they truly gave their all. Second guessing is endless.

Mary felt that she had not *been* enough. Her ardent desire was to bring Jesus and Lazarus together. Surely she loved both of them enough that the healing meeting should occur. But perhaps her love was too laced with self-interest. She may not have prayed hard enough. Or her sinfulness may have tainted her prayers. If she had loved more, then Jesus would have come.

Even though we know better, our secret thoughts whisper that bad things happen to us because we are bad. Somehow, we deserve these losses. Otherwise our prayers would have been answered. So we question the purity of our faith and the ardor of our love. And we can always find some lack.

Ultimately though, Martha and Mary did not remain in self-blame. Both of them knew that the matter rested with Jesus. If he had come, if he had wanted to be there and made the effort, he certainly had the ability to prevent Lazarus from dying. We too may move from condemning ourselves to wondering why the assistance of God sometimes seems so randomly given. We realize that God could intervene if God purposed to do so. And there appears to be no immediate causal reason why God should not.

From such experiences is born the cry of faithful anguish, "Lord, if you had been here, my brother would not have died" (John 11:21, 32, NRSV). These are not the words of an unbeliever. They are wrung from hearts that believe that God has both the power and the disposition to heal us. Those who have faith enough to expect Jesus to do something are the most disappointed when it appears he has withheld his mercies. Jesus could have done something for Lazarus; he could have done something for our loved ones. "Lord, if you had been here, all this pain would not have been necessary."

Why Lazarus?

Jesus chose deliberately to delay his healing not for a stranger but for a dear friend. He allowed this loss for those whom he particularly loved. At first, this may seem strange to us. If we had limited time and resources, we would give first to our closest loved ones. The choice of Lazarus for this example surely increased Jesus' own pain and the sharpness of the accusations from Mary and Martha. And perhaps this is precisely why Jesus allowed this death to come to his friends.

Jesus knew he was going to raise Lazarus from the beginning. But here we have a glimpse of how fully he entered the reality of being human in a world where people die. Jesus had predicted earlier that he himself would rise after his crucifixion. So death would be conquered. At the same time, however, he knew that ordinary people would not fully realize that triumph of life until the "close of the age." So Jesus allowed himself to experience the losses that the rest of us all suffer. He felt the grief of the present moment.

When Jesus arrived in Bethany, Martha and Mary's accusations stung him deeply. The weight of living in a world where we are always losing loved ones crashed upon him. He looked fully at those who surrounded the two sisters, and he saw their distress. Our text tells us that he was deeply moved in body and soul. He was greatly disturbed in spirit. Physically and spiritually, then, Jesus was shaken by the grief he felt and beheld. Even knowing all he did about the Resurrection, the present suffering still mattered.

In this story we receive the shortest verse of the Bible, "Jesus wept." He cried for Lazarus. He cried for Mary and Martha. He cried, perhaps, for the death on the cross he knew he was facing. Jesus wept for men and women who struggle in a fog of neglect to find some bit of love, only to see it snatched away by untimely death. For all these, Jesus was moved to tears.

The Music of Sorrow

J. R. R. Tolkien is best known for his book *The Hobbit* and his trilogy, *The Lord of the Rings*. In a prelude to these stories, however, Tolkien wrote an account of the creation of the world. He likened creation to a great making of music. Tolkien's story parallels the Christian understanding of the creation and fall and perhaps can reveal the deeper meanings in the story of Lazarus.

Tolkien described how Ilúvatar, who is God, declared to his creating servants a mighty theme for the music that would bring forth the world. Ilúvatar then invited these angelic beings to adorn his theme with their own creativity. At first, this creation symphony filled the void with goodness.

The glory was marred, however, when one of the angelic beings began to make music not in keeping with the theme of Ilúvatar. He made music of his own devising and for his own glory. Other angelic beings joined him, and discord arose in a great uproar to contend with the music of Ilúvatar. A storm raged around the throne.

And then Ilúvatar stood. He

> lifted up his right hand, and behold! a third theme grew amid the confusion. . . . It seemed at first soft and sweet, a mere rippling of gentle sounds . . . but it could not be quenched, and it took to itself power and profundity. . . . [This new music of Ilúvatar] was deep and wide and beautiful, but slow and blended with an immeasurable sorrow, from which its beauty chiefly came.[1]

Thus was the world created, both Tolkien's and perhaps ours, neither out of music of pure joy and praise nor out of music of discord and sin. Rather, God wove a more beautiful theme from the sadness of vain glory. So it is that all living in the world is touched with the sorrow of loss. But out of that sorrow is a greater beauty, an unquenchable song.

Tolkien went on to say that, "the echo of that music runs

through all the veins of the world in sorrow and in joy; for if joyful is the fountain that rises in the sun, its springs are in the wells of sorrow unfathomed at the foundations of the Earth." [2]

Perhaps these passages from Tolkien can uncover the "music" in this story of Lazarus. There is an eternal life of God that underlies all creation. There is also a great sorrow, the sorrow of creatures who fell away, who made music of their own devising and the death that afflicted the world ever since. But in the wells of sorrow at the foundation of the world, there is other music—deeper, more profound, and more beautiful. Sorrow and death will be woven into God's theme, and in the end all creation will be restored.

Writing on the Heart

We cannot always hear the joy in this sad music or see death as a gift, the horizon leading to more life. Our losses now are so acute that we scarce can imagine the eternity that awaits. We live in the interim. The world is not yet set right. We wait and wait for God to act in final redemption. And in the meantime, people grow ill, grow old, perish. "Lord, if you had been here, my brother would not have died." That cry of faithful anguish acknowledges that the world is not yet as it should be. Yet some hope persists that Jesus can set it right. Faith says, "All shall be well." Daily living insists, "Nothing is right." We live in between those two statements.

And Jesus, in his great love for us, chose his dear friend to show us both the pain and the hope. It had to occur to one whom he especially loved. He felt the loss not of a stranger but of a friend. Lazarus died, and God wrapped in flesh felt in the shaking of his own body the pain of these interim days. Lazarus died, and it was awful: sorrow in the wells at the foundation of the world. Jesus wept.

He experienced that loss so that in these long centuries between Jesus' resurrection and the redemption of creation, we may cling to the knowledge that God feels our anguish. Jesus knew he was about to raise Lazarus; he knew death is a beginning, not an end; he knew that God makes all things new. But in the meantime, he allowed himself to feel the loss. He took to heart the accusation, "Lord, if you had been here, my brother would not have died." Jesus did not deny that accusation. He embraced it, cried over it, and finally gave his life in response. He feels our faithful anguish still.

When we write the story of Mary, Martha, and Lazarus on our hearts, we begin first with its sorrow. We claim the empathy of Jesus for our own condition. We bind his tears for them as tears for our losses. In this story, we discover that God understands our broken hearts. He accepts our cries of faithful accusation, and he stands with us in our grief. Not one tear is lost.

By identifying with Mary or Martha, we recognize that in the face of suffering we wrestle with whether we have been or done enough. Ultimately though, we learn from these women to leave the blame and take our broken hearts to God. There we find sympathy to help us through before hope is fully realized.

Notes

[1] J. R. R. Tolkien, *The Silmarillion* (Boston: Houghton Mifflin Company, 1977), 16–17.
[2] *Ibid*, 40.

Prayers of Identification

The Eastern Orthodox tradition skillfully links identification with characters in the Bible to the present-day worshiper. Such prayers are careful to give the scriptural stories their full integrity as events that occurred once and for all in space and time. Simultaneously, the Orthodox recognize that in the mystery of the "communion of saints" these characters are still available to us as friends and guides. Our lives are shaped by theirs. A revealing phrase from that style of worship states:

As thou wert present there, so likewise be thou present here.

I invite you to pray with Mary and Martha, linking your life to theirs. Though you begin with the words provided, I hope your own prayers will follow.

Blessed Jesus, you did not turn from Martha or Mary
When they pled their complaints before you.
You bore the accusation of your absence
With understanding and compassion.
So do not, I pray, reject me for these
Faithful cries of anguish. This life is hard!

You assured Martha that dead Lazarus would live
And told her of the need to trust.
So comfort me again in my broken heart
That you are the Resurrection and the life.
Exhort me to believe beyond what I can see.
When you saw Mary's grief and the tomb, you wept,

Though you knew you would soon raise him.
Oh, weep with me now for all this loss.
Though all shall be well, it is not yet, not yet!

Tune your heart to mine and mine to yours
That I may know I am not alone
When I look upon this torn and tattered world
And rail that nothing fits; it is not right.

Catch me up in your passion by the tomb
That I may see my rage and sorrow as but little squalls
In the storm of your love for the world.

Prayers of Binding

The ancient prayer of St. Patrick, as translated by Mrs. C. F. Alexander, begins with the phrase, "I bind unto myself today." The one who prays goes on to bind, or fasten on, to his or her life events from Christ's life, the virtues of God's good creation, and the abiding presence of the Spirit. These powers then stand between the worshiper and the forces of evil in the world. In the spirit of that prayer, we too may tie the words of Christ to ourselves. Much as we would buckle on our belts or clasp a necklace, we may fasten on Jesus' words.

St. Patrick's prayer, typical of prayers in the Celtic tradition, is rendered with a pleasant rhythm and a simple rhyme scheme. This makes it easy to remember. The phrases are all succinct. I have attempted to provide an example of a binding prayer in the style of Mrs. Alexander's translation. I invite you to pray it several times each day, to carry it with you, perhaps even to learn it as a way of fastening Christ's words from this story to yourself. Once again, I hope that your own prayers will grow from using these.

> I clasp to me our Lord who wept
> When Lazarus his friend had died.
> By faith, I see our tears are kept
> Within the heart of God who cried.

An Emblem for Faith

On the next page is a symbolic emblem that was created after reflection upon this story. I invite you to spend several moments meditating upon it. Consider the location of the event in a definite, real place. Ponder the words of scripture chosen from the story. Consider how they communicate something central about the event, and how they give meaning to life today. Reflect upon how the story is rendered through the art. Allow the emblem to carry the story's meaning to you.

Seven

❦

Coming Forth

Lord, how can man preach thy eternal word?
He is a brittle crazy glass:
Yet in thy temple thou dost him afford
This glorious and transcendent place,
To be a window, through thy grace.

George Herbert, "The Windows"

The story of Lazarus, Mary, and Martha is found in John 11:1-15 and John 12:1-11.

Lazarus sat back from the table and looked at the beloved faces around him. He felt as if we were seeing them for the first time. How dear Mary looked as she gave her full attention to each person who spoke. She was always so interested! It had been a long time since Lazarus appreciated the soft lines around her eyes. No wonder people fell in love with her.

He saw Martha moving to clear the dishes. She was rarely still. He looked at her hands as she picked up a bowl. They were worn from work. Then he turned his attention to her face and noticed how she looked at each person in a hasty assessment of anything that might be needed. He realized how her toils were all a labor of love.

And then there was Jesus. Lazarus had always loved him. Jesus was a friend. Lazarus had known from the start that Jesus was extraordinary. But until last week, Lazarus had no idea of the power within him. Tonight Lazarus saw a depth to Jesus' features that seemed to spring from another place. And now Lazarus thought he had a clue to where that place was.

These three were so precious to him. Lazarus was happy to be here; the energy of being well after a long illness still surged through him. The world seemed fresh and full of wonder. And there was an abiding sense of relief. A great storm had passed, and now his life was returning.

Still, Lazarus could not shake an underlying feeling of sadness. He thrilled to be back in the daylight world. And yet it appeared to be missing something vital. He had difficulty describing his perception. The closest he came was to say that everything appeared watery, thinner, as if this world were but a reflection in a murky pool. Most people, Lazarus understood now, thought the world was the world. They didn't realize that everything was just a shadow of some finer, brighter, more solid source.

Lazarus could not remember what he saw during the four days he was dead. But he could feel that he had been exposed to that other "country," which was the source of this one. That world continued to lend some of its luster to Lazarus's sight. He saw more clearly: people and the creation were both more fragile and more important than anyone realized.

And when Lazarus looked at Jesus, he was sure that Jesus knew about that other world. With a start, Lazarus perceived that Jesus carried the essence of that far country within him. That explained why Jesus seemed more like a person than other people, more real than anything else. He not only came from the source, he was the source!

Lazarus's mind began to spin. He was at the limits of his imagination. And all these perceptions gave Lazarus a feeling of detachment. As much as he wanted to be back, and as much as he loved his sisters, he felt now like an observer. He was on the outside looking in.

As he listened to the others, Lazarus tried again to understand what had happened to him. His thoughts went back to the last week. His memory was still spotty. He tried to piece together the events from the time he had taken sick.

He remembered the night he felt so exhausted. His work shouldn't have taken that much out of him. By morning the fever was raging. At one hour, he felt like he was burning up. Then, for another, nothing could make him warm. And he grew steadily weaker.

After two days, he woke believing he should be better. So he got of bed, only to fall immediately back. This was more than a common illness. Something was terribly wrong with him. Lazarus began to panic. What if he never recovered?

Lazarus remembered how Mary had stayed with him day and night. Whenever he opened his eyes, he saw her face leaning over his. As the fever sent his thoughts into bizarre regions of his mind, the warmth of Mary's hand was his anchor to life.

There were hours when his head cleared though his body remained weak. In those moments, he worried for his sisters. If he didn't get well, how would they live? They were past the usual age for marriage. Their parents were dead. Lazarus had no brothers to take up the responsibilities. He simply mustn't leave them. But he could not will himself to be better.

In the moments when he accepted his helplessness, Lazarus began to cry out in his prayers for Jesus. Before then, he had prayed as any faithful man would. But he had not thought of himself as being in the category of those who needed Jesus' care. He had never wanted to be a burden to Jesus, only a friend. The need of his sisters was too great, however, and Lazarus knew only Jesus could help.

He remembered the effort it took to whisper to Mary, "Jesus. Get Jesus." She calmed him immediately.

"Martha has already sent a messenger. He'll be here soon. Just hang on dear brother, and rest until he comes."

But Lazarus had no memory of Jesus' arrival. He tried to hang on. But every hour his strength ebbed lower. Lazarus remembered how even in the haze of illness, he could perceive how Mary and Martha grew increasingly agitated. They talked in worried voices. He could feel Mary holding his hand too tightly, squeezing and unsqueezing as if she were working a pump.

His sisters talked about him as if he were already gone. They thought he couldn't hear them. And over and over they lamented, "Jesus still hasn't come! What will we do?"

He tried to speak but could not make his lips move. He wanted to say, "I'm here! I'm still here. Don't let me go!" But then he could not even open his eyes. Lazarus called for Jesus without words. The face of his friend and his Lord hovered in his mind.

And then, when he could no longer even pray, Lazarus remembered feeling very peaceful. He felt as if he were wrapped in swaddling clothes. They were tight and warm. His mother was holding him. Everything was fine.

The next thing he remembered was the sound of stone scraping against stone. He heard a cry from a long way off, calling him back. Jesus was the one who had called. Lazarus tried to come as quickly as he could.

And then he realized that he was standing inside a cave. His eyes hurt from the sudden light. His arms and legs were wrapped tightly in strong cloth. Lazarus's chin was bound so closely that he could not open his mouth to speak. He wanted to ask someone to remove the cloths because he could hardly breathe. And he was so cold!

Everything smelled at first like aloe and myrrh, then suddenly like something putrid. There was a stench of decay, as from a large animal. With that in his nostrils, Lazarus realized where he was. He was in his own tomb, and Jesus was calling him to come out.

Hardly knowing how, he shuffled and hopped toward the entrance. Instantly, hands were unwrapping the cloths. Air filled his lungs. His skin began to feel warmer as the blood began to flow. The smell improved. And Lazarus began to notice who was present.

Jesus stood before him. He looked drawn, as if a great tide of emotions had passed through him. But when his eyes met those of Lazarus, he communicated that he understood where Lazarus had been.

Mary was on the ground, holding on to Jesus' feet. She jumped up and was the first to take hold of Lazarus's unwrapped flesh, covering him with kisses. Martha came next, wonder on her face. She pulled his head down to hers and whispered, "You're back! The Lord has brought you back to us!"

There was a crowd of others with astonished looks. Lazarus recognized some of them as relatives. They continued to keep their distance.

And then Lazarus returned his attention to Jesus. Who was this man who had come to him at last with such power in his voice? There was much they needed to discuss! Jesus returned Lazarus's gaze, and he smiled. Lazarus realized that Jesus too seemed glad to have him back. And more. Jesus seemed relieved about more than Lazarus. The joy on his face now seemed to communicate that something of vital importance had been confirmed. Lazarus longed to know more.

I still want to know more, he said to himself as his thoughts returned to the room where the four of them had gathered for dinner. He looked at Jesus again.

Mary had gotten up from the table and gone over to Jesus with a jar of perfumed ointment. She poured it on his feet and massaged it into his skin. The room was instantly filled with the rich, sweet fragrance of the nard.

Lazarus was struck by the contrast in odors. The tomb had been so rancid just before he went out. It reeked of death. This smell was like spring, promising love and life.

He began to see that his illness, his death, and even his living again did not merely concern himself. Jesus too would be making this passage. What had happened to Lazarus was the beginning of a promise of life as dear as the fragrance of Mary's ointment. In a world of weeping, Jesus was offering comfort. Facing his own death, he was blazing a trail of life.

Lazarus sat back and watched the love that flowed through

Mary. She was wiping Jesus' feet with hair now. It was this kind of love that saw people through death to life. Of course it was Mary who showed him that! Lazarus smiled and gave thanks that he was back.

Praying with Lazarus

As we continue to invite scripture to shape our lives, we continue to pray from the perspective of the Bible characters, in order that our identification with them might deepen. Try on these prayers as if they were your own, as if you were Lazarus. And then, I hope, you will be moved to compose your own prayers.

My friend, my Lord!
I wondered where you were until
In the glaring light of a new day,
I saw that you had never left me.

Gracious Lord, you let me go in love.
I am proof that the journey you soon undertake
Is open to all.
You called me back.

And so I live knowing that I will face death again.
There are those who hate my living.
They seek to kill me,
But I am unafraid.

Though they slay me, yet shall I praise you.
Whatever death the world contrives,
You have life to more than match.

So I will thank you for my dear ones,
And for my home. For every day in this world.
It is broken and sad and full of grief.

Its splendor is thinning but yet reflects,
However darkly, a world of wonders beyond.

I will train my eye for glimpses of this country,
Traces contained in every hour, along every road.

I will look for you with expectation
Around every turn.
Whether I live or die, I live and am yours.
Oh, my friend and my Lord,
Fare you well in your hour!
I wait to hear you call me forth once more.

An Emblem for Faith

On the next page is a symbolic emblem that was created after reflection upon this story. I invite you to spend several moments meditating upon it. Consider the location of the event in a definite, real place. Ponder the words of scripture chosen from the story. Consider how they communicate something central about the event, and how they give meaning to life today. Reflect upon how the story is rendered through the art. Allow the emblem to carry the story's meaning to you.

Lazarus, come forth

Bethany

Eight

❧❧❧

This Illness Is Not unto Death

But when thou dost anneal in glass thy story,
Making thy life to shine within
The holy Preacher's; then the light and glory
More rev'rend grows, and more doth win:
Which else shows wat'rish, bleak, and thin.

George Herbert, "The Windows"

The story of Lazarus as a physical possibility for us seems unlikely. Not many of us will see resurrection occur so literally,
though there are some who report near-death experiences.

There are those who have seen a loved one dead on the op-
erating table return to life. Most of us, however, will experience
the power of this concrete event in more spiritual, metaphorical
ways.

In those terms, we may know quite well what it is to be
"four days dead." There are various times in our lives when part
of us dies; and before something new emerges, we may well won-

der if we are not bound in grave clothes, shut up in a tomb, and written off by everyone as finished.

Lazarus in Our Youth

Consider the passages of adolescence. A young woman in college may experience firsthand the old adage, "A girl will give sex in hopes of getting love, and a guy will give love in hopes of getting sex." The couple dates for several months. He begins to pressure her. It really doesn't take much pushing. And suddenly she feels as if she has died. She has lost something precious. She feels hollow. Sex without commitment was not as advertised. She wonders how she will ever look her father in the eye again. What will happen to the comfortable familiarity she used to have with her mother? Now that she feels lost, will she hope to be found or despair and plunge more deeply into a depressing lifestyle? Alone in her room, she can almost hear the sound of stone scraping on stone as her tomb is closed. She lies in the dark, bound hand and foot in grave clothes.

Every young man has to reckon with what it means to have more power in his body than sense in his head. More hormones than scruples. More opportunities than restraints. Men know about the wound of adolescence, the mysterious passion and rage that seems to afflict nearly all of us.

And sometimes a young man gets in way over his head. He literally follows his urge to do something destructive. Once the damage is done, he wakes up to his life as if splashed with cold water. He realizes, "I am not a boy anymore. That part has died. But I do not yet live as a man. People look at me now with disappointment. I am not the guy they thought I was. I never was that guy anyway, only now they know, and the image is dead." The future closes in front of him like a stone in front of a tomb. It is a dark time in a young man's life when he can't be what he was but doesn't yet know what, if anything, he can become. There are only consequences hanging upon him, and it feels like death.

Lazarus in the Middle Years

In the fullness of years when one has a place in the world, a work to do, and often people to care for, the Lazarus death may still come. A man may fight a battle at work, stake his reputation on it, and lose. He suddenly becomes expendable, irrelevant— tomb material.

But one appearance of Lazarus can lead to another. The same man may then realize with a shock that he no longer has any true friends. He has spent years working, in his family and in his employment. All those easy relationships from school years have become memories. There is still the male banter at parties when the men and women typically, strangely divide upon arrival. There are the occasional trips to the woods or the golf course. But nothing that goes below the surface, nothing that touches his soul. Such a man may wake one morning in midlife with a profound sense of loneliness. Urgency strikes. He wonders, *What have I been doing? I've got to get back to life.* But he thrashes at the sheets and realizes he is all tangled up in grave clothes.

There are other tombs in the full years. A woman, as well as a man, may realize with a start that all her relationships are based on manipulation. She thinks, *People talk to me because I make them need me. They do things with me because I know how to get them to do it. I wield guilt like a sword. But no one chooses me just to choose me. In fact, I am so far gone in my manipulations that most people have written me off. If I stop trying to control everyone, I will end up alone. To others, I am already dead. I do not count as a person.*

People in midlife become Lazarus when they can no longer fight the depression that has been creeping around the edges of their lives. They feel dead inside. Empty. Nothing is fun anymore. Everything tastes like rags in the mouth—grave rags. The thought of lying down in the cold, dark tomb becomes a constant fascination.

A man may realize that for the third time in a month he has found a reason to go into the city on business, so he can stop at the Club. There, anonymously he hopes, he lives out a fantasy that the young woman on the stage finds him attractive, even with his thinning hair and growing paunch. But on the way home, he thinks of his wife, and he feels like he is four days past dead.

A woman may feel that she has lost her life long ago, trying to save her addicted husband. The name of the addiction doesn't matter: alcohol, rage, perfection, sex, pills. The fact is that he can't stop, and she can't get out of helping him go down this path to mutually assured destruction. Her old friends know the truth of Martha's words, "But, Lord, by now there is a stench around her."

Lazarus in Later Years

Lazarus appears in the older years as well when people face the loss of power in the world. A man or woman may realize,

"People have changed the way they look at me. They smile benignly now. My words do not carry the same weight they once did. People who are faster race to take my place. And I should care about that, but half the time I don't. People who can talk louder and hear better now make most of the decisions. Steadily, they are making me irrelevant. And I cannot remember just when people started treating me like I am already in the tomb."

And so there is the rising fear that one will be put away somewhere that is unfamiliar. A person may think, *If I do not hold myself together, I'll be in a place where nurses in white polyester suits talk to me like I'm five. Everything will smell like disinfectant. I won't be able to find my things or reach my friends.*

I need to get better, but the load of these years is so heavy. How do these young people run around so lightly when there is all this grief wrapping tighter and tighter around our hands and our feet? I dream at night of the sound of stone scraping upon stone. They are closing the cave, and I cannot move or shout loud enough to make them stop.

Lazarus lived centuries ago in the town of Bethany. He was a real person who was a close friend of Jesus. But he also makes regular appearances at every stage of our lives. We know very well what it is to be written off, to be bound up, to be sealed in the tomb, four days dead.

Death, though, was not the end of the story for Lazarus. Jesus said, "This illness is not unto death." Though Lazarus died, he lived again. And we too may discover that life can succeed death in every stage. Every time there is a death, literal or symbolic, there is the possibility of resurrection to new life. Jesus cried in a loud voice, "Lazarus, come forth!" And he says it to us as well.

Writing on the Heart

Calling Forth Life at Every Stage

We saw how the Lazarus who dies comes to visit. Perhaps we can imagine how Jesus who calls forth Lazarus might address the same people.

Young woman, your life is not over. You do not have to continue what you have begun. My love for you has not changed. My will for you has not changed. My intention of joy for your life remains. You do not have to go spinning down a road of despair over what you have done or have been tempted to do. Come forth from that tomb. I am the Resurrection and the life. There is new life the other side of this death.

Young man, your innocence has died but not your soul. The bystanders have mourned your passing. They rolled a stone over your future, believing your crashing disappointment to be the end of you. It is not so! I am the Resurrection and the life. I am telling a story in you. I have work for you to do. Come forth!

Listen now, you woman, you man, smelling the rot of your life in the stale dark air of the cave you have hewn for yourself. I am the way, the truth, and the life. I can neither be bought, nor can I be lost by neglect. I cannot be manipulated. You can neither make me love you, nor can you keep me from loving you. You can neither earn my love, nor prevent it by anything that you do. You are not that powerful. Yes, the old life of guilt and control, manipulation and pandering secrets is dead. But behold, you still live. By my own choosing, I love you. You are my child. I have companionship for you that will satisfy you thoroughly. Come forth! I will fill your loneliness with my presence. I can teach you to love. Unbind those grave clothes and come out!

Aging man, aging woman, you are a newborn baby in my

arms. I am the ancient of days, the beginning and the end, the first and the last. I have known you from all eternity and have given you life that goes on forever. Your days on this earth are but a night's watch in my kingdom. But even now, this illness is not unto death.

You have great power yet in the world. You alone are old enough to have time to pray. How my scattered children need the love and peace of your prayers. You alone have time enough for all their little ones. They need your stories and your wisdom. They need one like you who has time to look at them and hear about their lives. I know your body pains you. This suffering shall not last for long. But for now I have need of you in this world. Come out of that tomb!

Writing on the Heart

Christ calls each of us forth to new life. At any stage in life, we may think we've reached the end of the line. And truly one part of living may be dying. Yet something in us goes on even in the worst suffering. It is not the end of our lives even if the world puts us to death, literally or spiritually. The present illness, no illness, is unto final death. Jesus remains the Resurrection and the life.

We can begin to bind this hope to ourselves as we first identify where a dying Lazarus has made his most recent appearance. When have those around you seemed to have mourned your passing or counted you as irrelevant? In what areas do you feel immobilized by the grave clothes bound around your hands, feet, and face? How does life seem to be stuck; how does life seem to be over?

With the awareness of such death firmly faced, we look for the presence of Jesus at the tomb. He cries over our pain. But more. We listen for the voice of Jesus who says, "Come forth!" What assurances of new life might he be giving? What possibilities for a new beginning exist? We can claim his words to Lazarus as words to us. And when the many deaths around us want to pull us into despair, we can say aloud Jesus' words, "I am the resurrection and the life. Those who believe in me, even though they die, will live" (John 11:25-26, NRSV).

This Illness Is Not unto Death

Prayers of Identification

The Eastern Orthodox tradition skillfully links identification with characters in the Bible to the present-day worshiper. Such prayers are careful to give the scriptural stories their full integrity as events that occurred once and for all in space and time. Simultaneously, the Orthodox recognize that in the mystery of the "communion of saints" these characters are still available to us as friends and guides. Our lives are shaped by theirs. A revealing phrase from that style of worship states:

As thou wert present there, so likewise be thou present here.

I invite you to pray with Lazarus, linking your life and experiences of spiritual death to his. Though you begin with the words provided, I hope your own prayers will follow.

Blessed Jesus, I am thankful
That you wept when Lazarus had died.
So all our griefs are known to you.
Even more, I am grateful
That you called him forth to life.
For many times I have watched others keep their distance.
The stench of death seemed upon me.
They deemed me finished and wanted to keep it that way.
I have felt the tight wrappings of grave clothes.
I have heard stone scrape on stone
And seen the blind darkness of the tomb.

117

O Lord, when I am unable to help myself,
Grant me the grace you gave to Lazarus.
Bid others brave the smell and open the tomb.
Call me by name to life.
Bid others unbind me head to toe
And see the new creation you have given me.

Gracious Jesus, you are the Resurrection
And the life.
Teach me to live again.

Prayers of Binding

The ancient prayer of St. Patrick, as translated by Mrs. C. F. Alexander, begins with the phrase, "I bind unto myself today." The one who prays goes on to bind, or fasten on, to his or her, life events from Christ's life, the virtues of God's good creation, and the abiding presence of the Spirit. These powers then stand between the worshiper and the forces of evil in the world. In the spirit of that prayer, we too may tie the words of Christ to ourselves. Much as we would buckle on our belts or clasp a necklace, we may fasten on Jesus' words.

St. Patrick's prayer, typical of prayers in the Celtic tradition, is rendered with a pleasant rhythm and a simple rhyme scheme. This makes it easy to remember. The phrases are all succinct. I have attempted to provide an example of a binding prayer in the style of Mrs. Alexander's translation. I invite you to pray it several times each day, to carry it with you, perhaps even to learn it as a way of fastening Christ's words from this story to yourself. Once again, I hope that your own prayers will grow from using these.

I bind unto myself this day
The one who said "Take the stone away.
Unbind that one and let him go!
Through life, the love of God is known."

An Emblem for Faith

On the next page is a symbolic emblem that was created after reflection upon this story. I invite you to spend several moments meditating upon it. Consider the location of the event in a definite, real place. Ponder the words of scripture chosen from the story. Consider how they communicate something central about the event, and how they give meaning to life today. Reflect upon how the story is rendered through the art. Allow the emblem to carry the story's meaning to you.

Nine

❧

Unless I See

Each verse doth shine.

George Herbert, "The Holy Scriptures (2)"

The story of Thomas is found in John 20:19–29; also 11:16; 14:5.

Why do you believe in him? Because of what you have heard? or felt? or read? I am amazed that you can believe without having seen him. I know about the doubts you must have. There are those panic moments when you wonder, *How do I know any of this is true? What if someone just made it all up?* If I were in your position, I would not have been able to continue following Jesus, as much as I loved him. I more than sympathize with any difficulties you have.

Though my doubts were not uncommon, my situation was unique. I received the tangible, physical proof for which I asked. You will probably never be given such a gift. But I would like to tell you my story in hope that it will be of some help to you. Jesus satisfied the doubts of one literal-minded, hard-headed skeptic. I would like you to find in me the beginnings of answers to your questions.

I was a fisher from the north country. I knew what it was to live in a rhythm of life contrary to that of most people. While others slept, we worked all night on the sea. The labor was difficult but satisfying. Time after time we would cast heavy nets into the water and then haul them in to see what we had caught. Many nights we cast dozens of times with barely a basket of fish to show for it. Other nights, if you had been awake, you would have heard our shouts across the water as we rejoiced in a rich take. At daybreak, we returned home with muscles aching and our bodies wet with chill in the dawn air.

Each morning there were nets and fish to be cleaned, gear to be stored, and deals to be made with merchants for our haul. Then, just as the world was returning to daily life, we made our way home and tried to sleep.

I knew what it was to work long and hard, expending the strength of my body for the survival of my family. We got by, but there was little extra. I lived without great expectations that my lot in life would ever change. Toil would be my portion until I was too weak to continue. Always there would be the Romans, pillaging our country with their taxes. And none of us ever expected to gain any status in the eyes of our leaders so bent on a purity no working man could maintain.

My hands were rough and covered with scars. The odor of sea and fish was ever about me. And my face was weathered by wind and rain. People knew what I did without having to ask.

There was a pride among us fishers. We were content to be different than others. Independence became as much a part of life as the wide horizon and the bob of the boat. We would never be rich or powerful, but we would be free. As fishers, we felt we knew the meaning of hard work as well as anyone. We knew what was what in the world. Each of us had endured storms, seasons of futility, days of catches too many to sell, and the distance given to us by others for our ways.

I never expected to leave my trade. Nor did I intend to become "religious." Jesus changed that. When he was just a rumor to me, he earned my respect by his willingness to be with ordinary people. Then I began to sense his power when he healed Simon's mother-in-law. The Great Catch confirmed it.

I wasn't there the morning he sent Simon and the others out to drop their nets again. The news of their haul spread through town like fire. I saw the catch on the beach. In all my years of fishing, there had never been anything like this. I wouldn't have believed that the Sea of Galilee held so many, let alone that they could all be caught in one cast of the nets. But I saw the boats overflowing with fish. The nets were swollen to the breaking point.

I wanted to know how they had managed to get the catch to shore. But Simon and the others were not to be seen. The fish were free for the taking. The market would be flooded now. No one would need fish for days. I was stunned to see that they had been so careless with their equipment and their produce. Their livelihoods lay abandoned on the shore. The gossip said they had left it all to follow Jesus.

It was not long before Jesus called me. I'm almost embarrassed at how easy it was for him. I had thought that I would bow my head to no man. But when I heard him speak my name and ask me to join him, there was no decision. Here was a man like no other, with power to create change in the world and a plan to do it. I followed him immediately.

As the days turned into months, my loyalty to him grew absolute. He healed our people of their diseases; he emboldened them to grasp hold of their lives even amidst the Romans and the Pharisees. And I felt his power flow through my own hands the afternoon we fed five thousand with five loaves and two fish. He gave himself through us; and as we handed out the food, abundance splashed all around.

Jesus became to me the mystery behind the invisible wind that races across the water. He was the depth in the sea and the radiance in the sun. All the strength of muscle and blood that I had ever felt course through me in the pride of my work found its origin in him. My life was his.

So when the message came that Lazarus was ill, I was prepared to go to Bethany with Jesus. I knew, though, that trouble lay down that path. The chief priests hated Jesus. His popularity had grown until they were in a panic over him. I knew those people; they would not sit quietly by while their profitable, fragile alliance with Rome was threatened. If we neared Jerusalem, there would be confrontation.

I had hoped we could avoid a fight for as long as possible. We did not have the strength to survive their muscle. But if Jesus said we had to go there, I would be by his side. *Come on then*, I thought, *we're not afraid*. There was no reason to pretend; death lay ahead, but I had never been one to cower in the face of reality. I said to the others, "Let us go too that we may die with him."

Within a matter of days the storm came. Judas betrayed our location. A band of official thugs came with their weapons to arrest Jesus. At first I thought he would turn them away. They fell back at his words. But Jesus seemed to accept their demand; he offered himself willingly to them and asked that we be set free.

Simon beat me to drawing a sword and slashed at one of the

men. I was ready to fight now. But Jesus forbade any further conflict. He let them lead him away.

Immediately all the courage left me. I am ashamed to say it, but I ran. I had been ready to die with him, but in the moment when there was no way for me to help, I just wilted like a boy on his first night at sea.

For the next three days, we huddled in the room we had rented for Passover. All of us were far from home, and we didn't know what to do. The others clung to that place for comfort. But I was too restless to stay there long. I had to get out. Walk. Think. Try, somehow, to figure out how to carry on.

For me the loss was final and complete. I was shattered. Everything I had believed about Jesus was worthless. The dream of a new world had died with him.

My old beliefs returned. The world was the way the world was, and nothing about it would change. Reality was terrible, but it had to be faced. I would go on. At least I wouldn't give them the satisfaction of giving up. I would go back to work. I would get by.

By the time the news of the Resurrection reached me, the cynical shell had already hardened in me. I would not be taken again by wild hopes. I couldn't imagine why they were making up such stupid stories. Now it seemed as if I was to be cut off even from my friends. But I simply could not join their delusion.

"Look," I said. "Unless I see the nail holes in his hands and put my finger in them, I won't believe you. Unless I can put my hand in the side where the spear pierced him, I won't buy your story. He's dead, stabbed, hung on a tree. Grasp the truth. It's over."

More than a week passed, and nothing happened. Their resurrected Jesus never appeared. I stayed with them now not only because I had no place to go, but because I hoped to help the others accept the reality that Jesus was gone.

I had no preparation for what occurred. We were in the room with the doors locked, simply brooding. And there was Jesus. "Peace be with you," he said. Then he turned to me.

"Thomas, put your finger here, and see my hands." I looked at his outstretched palms and saw the holes where the nails had been. They were just beginning to heal. "Put out your hand and place it in my side." He pulled up his robe, and I could see the open wound where the spear had pierced him. "Don't be faithless any longer, but believe!" He waited for me to touch him.

But his voice was enough. It still commanded my soul. His appearance was enough. I wanted to touch him, yes, but not to confirm that he was really here. I wanted to embrace my master.

Words, stronger than I had ever said, leapt from my mouth, "My Lord and my God!" After a few more moments he was gone.

I had asked for impossible proof, trying to get the others to live in reality. And then Jesus gave me more than the impossible. He appeared and was more real than he had ever been. He was there.

We saw him another time before he departed this earth. He cooked breakfast for us on the beach. I watched him tend a fire and eat fish and bread. Jesus who had died lived again, in that body, in this world.

I know that you will struggle to believe me. I could not believe the others. I did not want to believe; I did not want to see beyond my loss. I have told you my story as one skeptic to another. I speak as one who knew a hard life that got harder and as one who always tried to face reality squarely. I was not the big, bounding puppy that Peter was, ready to accept it all. I was not the lover that John was, nor did I ever have the vision of Mary Magdalene. I was a fisher who found for a while someone who was more powerful than the sea I rode upon or the wind by which I sailed. I lost him and was prepared to leave it at that.

But he did not leave me there. He appeared to me. He called my name again. The world is not always as it seems. The lines are not irrevocably drawn for us. He lives. And so anything is still possible. I know, because I have seen.

You do not see. And you have known loss enough to harden the eyes of your heart. You cannot touch him, and you have seen brokenness enough to expect little more. I will not be able to convince you. But I have told you my story and wish that it would help. For this one hard-headed doubter, and so perhaps for all, Jesus showed himself fully. He still lives.

Praying with Thomas

As we continue to invite scripture to shape our lives, we continue to pray from the perspective of the Bible characters, in order that our identification with them might deepen. Try on these prayers as if they were your own, as if you were Thomas who refused to believe until he saw the risen Christ. And then, I hope you will be moved to compose your own prayers.

My Lord and my God!
I could not believe,
And I am ashamed now.

You know me altogether.

Wind and sea, nets and boats,
Were my world.
I was no one's fool and
Followed no one's dreams but my own.

Until you appeared and called my name.

With all my life and soul I believed in you.
I was ready to die with you,
But you did not let me.
Instead you allowed them to take you away,
And my belief died.
Childlike faith met the real world.
I wondered how I could have trusted you.

I expected nothing more again
But the strain of the catch
And the steady struggle with the water.

Until you appeared and called my name,
Once again.

And I cannot help myself.
I believe.
Your course was sure all along but
The storm blinded me to it.

Oh my Lord, thank you for not giving up on me
As easily as I did on you.

By the prints in your hands I will live.
By the wound in your side I will carry on.

I need nothing more.

An Emblem for Faith

On the next page is a symbolic emblem that was created after reflection upon this story. I invite you to spend several moments meditating upon it. Consider the location of the event in a definite, real place. Ponder the words of scripture chosen from the story. Consider how they communicate something central about the event, and how they give meaning to life today. Reflect upon how the story is rendered through the art. Allow the emblem to carry the story's meaning to you.

Ten

❧

Those Who Have Not Seen

O that I had deep cut in my hard heart
Each line in thee!

Henry Vaughan, "H. Scriptures"

The story of Thomas carries us right to our own difficulties with belief. Here we face the very struggle with scripture that has occasioned this book. We do not see Jesus in the flesh. We cannot touch him. Thomas is an ally for all who have lived in seasons of doubt. He could not embrace the Resurrection just by the stories of his friends alone. Direct experience is what he craved and received.

So Thomas is at once attractive and distant to us. We resonate with his need but do not receive the confirmation that he did. Rather, we are left with Jesus' provocative words, "Have you believed because you have seen me? Blessed are those who have not seen and yet have come to believe" (John 21:29, NRSV). This saying carries the promise of blessing for all who must rely on the witness of the disciples and not personal experience. Yet the blessing is elusive. My own heart cries, "But I still want to see!"

Earlier on, we considered how the story of Lazarus provides an anchor to hope when we are tossing in a sea of loss. By connecting with Jesus' response to Mary and Martha, we can perceive that Jesus weeps for a world that has not yet been set right. His raising of Lazarus is a model for ways we can experience resurrection in many areas of our lives. It is as if this story were left for those of us in the interim between the days when Jesus walked the earth and the day when he will come again. We have speculated that Jesus allowed his dear friends to experience these agonies precisely so that he could fully enter the cycle of life and death in the world. These characters stand as an example for us.

Now we will struggle to see if Thomas is also a character who provides a model for us who believe in this interim time. It is possible that Jesus deliberately chose to appear to the other disciples when Thomas was absent in order that Thomas might be a forerunner for all of us who were not there.

Thomas captures the feelings we have of missing out on the kind of closeness to God that others seem to possess. He wasn't there; he missed it. And we may feel that too many times we did not enter the great moment of worship that others had one Sunday. The rest of our study group was energized by their insights from a biblical text, but we were blind to new meanings. We feel stupid in our prayers and for all the good it does, we might as well be reading the phone book instead of the Bible in our devotions.

To this point, I have tried to help you enter the feelings of the Gospel stories in such a way that you can identify analogous feelings in daily life. By examining the internal dynamics of the stories, we can discern similar dynamics in us. And hopefully, once we locate ourselves somewhere along the story line, we can be moved along by the rest of the story into transformation.

With the stories of the man by the pool and Lazarus, we have been seeking interior correspondence rather than literal healing or a physical resurrection from the dead. And it is doubtful that any of us will ever face the literal stoning that was an imminent danger to the woman caught in adultery. We connect with her indirectly by relating to the experience of being caught and facing the judgment of others. The characters and events from the Gospel stories provide metaphors for our daily lives. After working with the narratives, we are able to understand what it means to experience a "Lazarus death" or hear the pointed question "Do you want to get well?"

The Spiritual Experience of Thomas

In the same way, we may search for experiences that correspond to Thomas's encounter with the risen Christ. We know that it is highly unlikely that any of us will receive a personal visit from the physical Jesus. But there are those who say they have received all the confirmation of Jesus' reality that they could ever need.

There are moments when the veil of doubt is lifted and people experience the confirming presence of God. This may occur during the wonder of childbirth or in the mysterious peace that arrives while standing by a graveside. Others might "see" God while sailing on swelling waves or hiking through mountains. Some people receive affirming dreams that change them from doubters to believers. Some gain a sense of revelation while reading the Bible. During the intimacy of love or the quiet of prayer, the sense of the everlasting presence may come. Others discover during a session of therapy the sudden, loving embrace of Christ. In whatever form the experience arrives, from deep within the soul comes the impulse to affirm in response, "My Lord and my God."

Following Thomas, we might take some time to consider what our demands for proof of God's love entail. Thomas did not ask for anything that the other disciples had not already received. So he was not asking for favors but only to be caught up with the rest. What kinds of experiences have you heard about in others' lives that you long to have? And then, we have to wonder, if all we seek were given to us, would that be enough to make us believe wholeheartedly? Are we willing to be so overwhelmed with God's reality that the confession "My Lord and my God!" rushes out of our hearts and mouths?

Of course we cannot dictate to God when such confirming experiences will occur. Thomas had to wait for his. But we can become aware of how to get ourselves in the places that most attune our senses to God. Another way to say this is that we can learn how to get in the way of God so that should God pass through, we do not miss the visit.

If you were really serious about having a Thomas experience, I would invite you to leave familiar surroundings for a few days. Go alone, and plan not to be too busy or too distracted with activity. Then, seek to discover what it is you miss. Leave time on this retreat for your heart to do its work. Feel again what you deeply love. Then you could ponder the mystery of that love. Why is there such a hole in your heart when you are absent from that person, that place, or that community? In the feeling of loneliness, you may discover the depth of your love; and in the ache of that love, you might feel the presence of God that answers all doubt.

Or I could ask you to go out into the woods or a garden. Put your hands in the earth. Feel the cool, rich dirt. Kneel down and look closely at the tiny plants and wildflowers. Then look up at the leaves in the trees high above. Do not look with greeting card eyes that say, "Isn't that lovely!" before you have truly received the sight. Rather, look in a way that is still and time-consuming and thoughtful. Listen to the sound of the wind in the boughs. Smell the scent of the plants as they make their wonderful exchange for the oxygen we need. Consider how year after year the flower returns to live for just a few weeks, then is gone. Beyond its biological function, what purpose does it have but beauty—beauty in itself—whether any person sees it or not. Consider the trees, which are constant, rooted, reaching. On such an afternoon of using your senses, you might feel the presence of God, answering your doubts.

By reading this book, you have already been seeking the presence of God in scripture and in prayer. Have you felt any confirmation of faith? Have you lingered with the characters and received Jesus' words as addressed to you? Through such work, it is possible to experience God.

Thomas Remains Elusive

All of these activities are valid and desirable. We could wrap things up neatly now. Each story would have been "spiritualized" into a palatable form. But Jesus' words in this last story seem to point away from that internal direction. He seems to want us to understand God as not only within, but without. There is an objective, once-and-for-all dimension to the life of Christ as recorded in scripture. This quality gives boundaries to our work with the Gospels and provides form for our experiences of faith.

In the method of study used in this book, we have attempted to take the Gospel stories inside ourselves as we work with them. Our own experience has come into play as we discovered the ways in which we *are* the lame man by the pool, the woman caught in a circle of condemnation, the sisters wondering why Jesus did not come when he was needed. We located where we were in the narrative train of the story and hoped that by hopping on board we might be moved along just as the Gospel characters were.

Identifying with the characters in this way, however, we may have begun to think that the characters are part of us. They can be construed as aspects of ourselves. In this switch, we may believe that we are the source of the characters; that all this work is internal and purely spiritual. And so we may be tempted to set our own terms for the stories, leaving the boundaries provided by the biblical texts. In such a case, we may profitably use the stories for meaning and energy, but we lose contact with the Christ of history and so miss the deepest transforming power. We may end up shaping the stories, and not they us.

The story of Thomas pulls us back from such spiritualizing. Jesus' words to him remind those who come after that the events described in the Gospels occurred in the material world at a point in history involving real people. And they occurred only once.

Their meaning endures; their internal dynamics are repeated; they continue to serve as conduits for the grace of the living, ever renewing God. But nevertheless, they resist being collapsed into present experience only.

There is an essential kernel of story that always remains "other," no matter how closely we identify with it. The stories may live inside us, but they are never wholly within. They have a location without. Similarly, God dwells within us, but that is not only where God is. God is without and can never be contained in human terms.

Writing on the Heart

The goal of this work has been to create conversations at the deepest levels between our lives and the lives of those characters in the stories, between our depths and God. These exchanges may occur in the interior regions of the soul, but they can never be fully contained within us. "Deep calls to deep," as the psalmist says. God who is within us is also always outside of us. We are called, ultimately, to move out of ourselves, albeit from our very centers, in worship of God.

The very exteriority of the stories prevents us from diluting them. They remain a constant challenge. We invite them to shape us, and we struggle not to reshape them into our image. We realize that we are called to submit to the demands of the stories and so to the will of God. In this way we have real possibility for abundant growth. By maintaining our respect for the integrity of the stories, we are not left to wallow alone in our own thoughts and habits. We have real help to become more than we presently are.

Jesus' words in the Thomas story stop us from too much internalizing. He seems to recognize that a story will be told about this event. Within the story he says, "You believed because you have seen." Extending beyond the event to those who would hear of it for generations, he says, "Blessed are those who believe though they have not seen." It is as if he turns to the camera and says to the invisible audience, "You are not here to see this directly, but you are blessed if you believe from your distance."

We will never have Thomas's exact experience, but we have his story. We can follow the process of writing it on our heart. I can imagine being Thomas. And so I can sense how he was the doubter for all of us who would doubt later. I feel how left out he was and resonate with how hard it is to believe. Then I can imagine how wonderful it was for Thomas to stare with wide eyes at the pierced hands of Jesus who was crucified but lived again.

Then to my imagination, I add my own struggles with doubt. I recall the times when I have felt left out of spiritual experiences. And I add the memory of any moments I have had when the presence of God was confirmed to me. I listen for the precious times when my life corresponded to the story. Such connections are thrilling.

But Thomas leads me further. The story is not just about my personal, interior experiences. It's about acknowledging the reality of the resurrected Jesus. The story leads beyond myself and into worship. I bind on the words of Thomas. They become my own. Through Thomas I too can cry out, "My Lord and my God!"

Thomas saw and believed in his resurrected Lord because

Jesus showed himself to Thomas. We learn from his story that what we can know of God through the Bible comes not only by the passion of our desire or the quality of our study technique; we receive God through the scriptures ultimately because God graciously chooses to be known to us in that way. Even the faith we have is a gift from God. There is, then, an element of mystery contained in all reading of scripture. We try to get as close as we can, to understand as deeply as we are able, to draw all the connections that are possible. But finally, God is the one who makes it possible for us to find meaning and life through the stories. It is God who writes the words on our hearts.

Prayers of Identification

The Eastern Orthodox tradition skillfully links identification with characters in the Bible to the present-day worshiper. Such prayers are careful to give the scriptural stories their full integrity as events that occurred once and for all in space and time. Simultaneously, the Orthodox recognize that in the mystery of the "communion of saints" these characters are still available to us as friends and guides. Our lives are shaped by theirs. A revealing phrase from that style of worship states:

As thou wert present there, so likewise be thou present here.

I invite you to pray with Thomas, linking your life to his. Though you begin with the words provided, I hope your own prayers will follow.

Oh, you who did not rebuke Thomas
For his absence nor leave him alone in his doubt,
So do not cease your revelations to me,
For I am dull and hard-headed, too often
Outside the room when others see.

You gave to Thomas what he needed,
You adjured him to be faithless no more,
So encourage me, and help me see that all I need
Has already been given.

You received his confession
And projected his faith toward others

Who could not be there,
So give me the blessing of lips
Which express the heart that shouts,
My Lord and My God!

Prayers of Binding

The ancient prayer of St. Patrick, as translated by Mrs. C. F. Alexander, begins with the phrase, "I bind unto myself today." The one who prays goes on to bind, or fasten on, to his or her life events from Christ's life, the virtues of God's good creation, and the abiding presence of the Spirit. These powers then stand between the worshiper and the forces of evil in the world. In the spirit of that prayer, we too may tie the words of Christ to ourselves. Much as we would buckle on our belts or clasp a necklace, we may fasten on Jesus' words.

St. Patrick's prayer, typical of prayers in the Celtic tradition, is rendered with a pleasant rhythm and a simple rhyme scheme. This makes it easy to remember. The phrases are all succinct. I have attempted to provide an example of a binding prayer in the style of Mrs. Alexander's translation. I invite you to pray it several times each day, to carry it with you, perhaps even to learn it, as a way of fastening Christ's words from this story to yourself. Once again, I hope that your own prayers will grow from using these.

I fasten the cry of Thomas to me.
He saw the wounds, he heard the word;
To him it was given to see.
With him I join, "My God, my Lord!"

An Emblem for Faith

On the next page is a symbolic emblem that was created after reflection upon this story. I invite you to spend several moments meditating upon it. Consider the location of the event in a definite, real place. Ponder the words of scripture chosen from the story. Consider how they communicate something central about the event and how they give meaning to life today. Reflect upon how the story is rendered through the art. Allow the emblem to carry the story's meaning to you.

Appendix

❧✦❧

About the Sources

In *Writing on the Heart*, I have drawn from three very deep wells of spiritual nourishment. As you have worked with the Gospel stories, your interest may have grown in learning more about these sources. Succinctly, the sources are these:

1) The Prayer Style of the Eastern Orthodox Church

The prayers in the worship of the Orthodox churches evoke a sense that the characters and the events of the Bible are immediately accessible to us. A Gospel event is both a literal, concrete event that occurred once in history as well as a present drama unfolding upon the stage of worship. The ones who pray interact with those characters and identify their lives with the Gospel figures. In worship, the people from the Bible are still very much alive to us.

For example, in the case of the healing of the paralytic (found in Luke 5:17-26), the Orthodox prayer reads as follows:

By Thy divine intercession, O Lord, as Thou didst raise up the paralytic of old, so raise up my soul, paralyzed by sins and thoughtless acts; so that being saved I may sing to Thee: Glory to Thy majesty, O Bountiful Christ![1]

The identification is spiritual. This man in the Gospels was paralyzed, and Christ raised him. In worship, each member of the congregation may ask, "How am I paralyzed?" The answer to the prayer is by habitual "sins and thoughtless acts." The solution to the problem shared by the worshiper and the paralytic of old is to ask Christ for healing. The effect of the prayer is to say, "O Christ, raise me up from the paralysis of soul that keeps me bound in the same old patterns." And the result is the praise of our "Bountiful Christ."

As noted throughout the book, the watchword for the Orthodox way of identification in prayer is "As thou wert present there, so likewise be thou present here." When the people from the Gospels take the stage in the drama of worship, we join them in the scene. Thus, our own lives can be moved through the play as theirs were. In effect, we hitch our lives to the people in the Gospels and so get moved from being stuck or disabled to being transformed and healed.

Building on this style, I have tried to invite you to enter imaginatively into the lives of those Gospel characters we are studying. We have attempted to feel their emotions both before and after their encounter with Christ. I have tried to provide prayers in words they might have used, thus linking our souls to theirs. The more we can enter their lives, the more we can find these characters unfolding in our daily lives.

2) The Binding Prayer of St. Patrick

The ancient prayers preserved from the Scottish Highlands share a continuous invitation to God to be part of every moment of every day. The worshipers invoke God's presence in even the most mundane activities. One of the most powerful prayers from that spiritual tradition is known as "St. Patrick's Breastplate." Mrs. C. F. Alexander has translated it with evocative power and memorable rhythm. It begins,

> I bind unto myself today
> The strong name of the Trinity,
> By invocation of the same,
> The Three in One and One in Three.
>
> I bind this day to me for ever,
> By power of faith, Christ's Incarnation;
> His baptism in the Jordan River;
> His death on cross for my salvation;
> His bursting from the spicèd tomb;
> His riding up the heavenly way;
> His coming at the day of doom;
> I bind unto myself today.[2]

The one who prays seems to be fastening on the life and works of Christ. Praying in this way goes beyond identifying with the people Jesus met. It means taking as your own the words he spoke to them and the actions he performed toward them.

Continuing our example of the paralytic, we might say, "I bind to myself Christ's words to the man on his bed, "Friend, your sins are forgiven." As he said the words to the paralytic, he said them to me. I fasten this declaration to myself. I will learn it, ponder it, recite it, and each time claim it as my own. I will embrace Jesus' healing power, which enabled the man to get up and walk. Wherever and whenever I am paralyzed, I will speak Christ's healing forgiveness into that illness.

Building upon St. Patrick's prayer, I have provided "Prayers of Binding" for you to use as part of your work with the Gospel passages. Hopefully, such exercises enabled you to have a much easier time remembering what you have read in the Gospels and taking the meaning of your encounter with scripture further during the day.

3) The Gospel Medallions from the Cathedral of St. John the Divine

Along the floor of the center aisle of the Cathedral of St. John the Divine in New York City are nine emblems commemorating events from the life of Christ. The medallions are made of raised brass upon circles of polished granite, each about three feet in diameter. At the top of each circle is the name of the place in Israel where the event occurred. Around the circle are words from the story that communicate a central meaning. And in the middle of the circle is a symbolic representation of the meaning of the event.

The emblems are striking in the way in which they communicate both the historical and eternal significance of the Gospel stories. Each one is located in a particular place, but each one is rendered in a way that points towards eternal significance. Ringing the circle are the words of Christ. These too are both particular and universal. They are significant in the historical moment and eternally valid.

Best of all, for me these medallions are visible and concrete. They render the stories in the world, off the page and for all to see. Artist Kelly Wood has worked in this style to produce the emblems found at the end of each chapter. Her goal has been to fashion the words of scripture into concrete symbols that we could take with us through the day.

The emblems provided for each story are for you to use in your own meditations, to take with you into the world, and, hopefully, to stimulate you to make your own concrete symbols. I am hopeful that you might try your hand at making emblems from the story. They can be drawn on paper, molded in and painted onto clay, or hammered into aluminum discs, to name a few media you might use. The end result is to have actual, literal reminders on our desks or in our pockets that recall the work we have done and urge us to go forward.

Notes

[1] From the liturgy for the Fourth Sunday after Pascha, taken from *The Divine Liturgy According to St. John Chrysostom*, (South Canaan, PA: St. Tikhon's Seminary Press, 1977), 191.

[2] Found in numerous sources:

The Hymnal of the Episcopal Church (New York: The Church Hymnal Corporation, 1940), 268.

The Book of Common Worship (Louisville, KY: Westminster/John Knox Press, 1993), 27.

David Adam, *The Cry of the Deer* (London: Triangle/SPCK, 1987), 6. U.S. Publisher: Wilton, CT: Morehouse Barlow.

Questions for Further Reflection for Individual or Group Use

The Healing at the Pool (John 5: 1-15)
Chapter One

1) Why did Jesus ask the man if he wanted to be well?

2) What does the man's reply indicate about what he felt about his illness and the possibilities for health?

3) Jesus told him to "Get up and walk." How many times is this phrase repeated in the biblical account? What does this command imply about what the man needs in order to gain access to the healing power?

4) Is the power for healing ever in question? What does that say about how healing "works"?

5) What difficulties will the man face now in his life of walking and being well? What danger will be readily at hand?

6) When Jesus found him later, he said, "See, you are well. Sin no more lest something worse befall you." In the context of this story, what would be sin for this man?

7) What does the pallet represent for the man? Why is it so important that he pick it up and take it with him?

Chapter Two

1) What patterns do we fall into after "thirty-eight years" of living in one particular way?

2) In what areas of your life have you felt disabled? When do you live the role of the invalid? Where have you been paralyzed for a long time?

3) For the man at the pool, the only possibility for healing seemed to be reaching the waters first upon their bubbling. How do we get caught in a limited vision of solutions?

4) What pallets, or tangible symbols of your invalidism, do you need to pick up? What might you need in order to take up your pallet and walk?

5) How is it that something worse can befall us after a few hours of being well? What is the new way to live?

The Woman Caught in Adultery (John 7:53–8:11)
Chapter Three

1) The teachers and Pharisees say, "The law commands us to stone such women." Look up Leviticus 20:10; Deuteronomy 22:22. What does the law say? What is the inequity here? What was the trap for Jesus?

2) Let us consider this woman. How does she feel "being made to stand before the crowd"? What does she imagine her future to be? What is going through her head in the immediacy of the moment?

3) How do you think the crowd was feeling at that time? the teachers and Pharisees?

4) Why do you think Jesus bent down to write in the ground? What are some of the possibilities for what he wrote?

5) How did Jesus' words cause the crowd to disperse?

6) Why does Jesus ask the woman where her accusers are? Why does he ask rhetorically "Does no one condemn you?" What effect might that have had on her?

Chapter Four

1) When are we caught as this woman was caught?

2) When are we swept up in condemnations of self or others? When do we get smugly self-righteous? What is fun about having a scapegoat?

3) What is the implication for the way we regard others in Jesus' words: "Let the one who is without sin cast the first stone"?

4) What does it take to transform you from a state of righteous anger to humble identification with someone's pain and sin?

5) What are we to do with Jesus' lack of condemnation? as accusers? as accused?

6) In what areas of your life might Jesus speak these words to you, "Let the one without sin cast the first stone"?

7) Where might Jesus want to say to you, "Neither do I condemn you"?

8) Compare "Neither do I condemn you" with "See, you are well." How do such statements create as well as describe transformation?

Lazarus, Mary, and Martha (John 11:1-44)
Chapter Five

1) Why did Jesus delay? What are the possibilities, and which ones seem most satisfactory to you?

2) What faith is behind Martha's statement "Lord, if you had been here, my brother would not have died"? What accusation?

3) What might be the differences in feeling or thought behind Mary and Martha's identical statements?

4) Why do you imagine Jesus answered Martha with theological assurances and Mary with tears?

5) Why did Jesus weep? The Greek word translated as "deeply troubled" can mean both anger and sorrow. What might have caused those two emotions in Jesus?

Chapter Six

1) In what ways have you experienced the "delay of God"?

2) When you find that you are blaming yourself for your own or someone else's suffering, does your guilt take on Martha's "I should have done more" or Mary's "I should have loved more"?

3) How do you make peace with such accusations?

4) Can you remember times when you dared to say to God, "Lord, if you had been here, Lazarus would not have died"?

5) During the times when you are waiting for God, how might Jesus' words help you, "This illness is not unto death"?

6) Jesus wept for Lazarus even though he knew he would raise him. How can that fact help you in dealing with loss?

Lazarus, Mary, and Martha (John 11:1-44; 12:1-11)
Chapter Seven

1) What might have been Lazarus' thoughts and feelings as the illness came upon him?

2) What changes might have occurred in Lazarus's prayers as the illness moved toward death?

3) Do you think Lazarus was pleased or reluctant to return to his life in Bethany?

4) What challenges do you imagine Lazarus faced with his new life?

5) How might Lazarus's view of life in the world have changed? How might his view of Jesus have changed?

Chapter Eight

1) In what ways are people "left for dead" at various stages and situations of life?

2) Martha worried that a stench would come from the tomb. In what ways do our "deaths" give off a stench that repels others?

3) What might the grave clothes mean symbolically? How can we help to unbind the grave clothes from people emerging into new life?

4) In what areas of your life would you most like to hear Jesus say, "_____, come forth!"

5) What joys and trials do you face as Christ's life grows within you?

Thomas (John 11:16; 14:5; 20:19-29)
Chapter Nine

1) What do we learn of Thomas from his brief appearance in the Lazarus story (John 11:16)?

2) What do we learn of Thomas from his brief appearance in the story of Jesus' final night (John 14:5)?

3) Why do you imagine Thomas was not with the others the evening Jesus first appeared?

4) Did he ask for more or less proof than the other disciples received?

5) Do you think Thomas actually touched Christ or was seeing enough? Check the text carefully and expand on your opinion.

Chapter Ten

1) What proof of Jesus would you most like to have?

2) What forms of assurance do we receive that confirm our faith?

3) Jesus said that those who have not seen are blessed. How do you experience this absence of the physical Christ as a blessing?

4) How appropriate and/or useful is it to make demands for experience along the line of Thomas?

5) In what ways can the skepticism of Thomas be a help to us now?